SEX SLAVES
AND SERFS

SEX SLAVES

AND SERFS

The Dynamics of Human Trafficking in a Small Florida Town

Erin C. Heil

FIRST**FORUM**PRESS

A DIVISION OF LYNNE RIENNER PUBLISHERS, INC. • BOULDER & LONDON

Published in the United States of America in 2012 by
FirstForumPress
A division of Lynne Rienner Publishers, Inc.
1800 30th Street, Boulder, Colorado 80301
www.firstforumpress.com

and in the United Kingdom by
FirstForumPress
A division of Lynne Rienner Publishers, Inc.
3 Henrietta Street, Covent Garden, London WC2E 8LU

Library of Congress Cataloging-in-Publication Data
Heil, Erin C.
  Sex slaves and serfs: the dynamics of human trafficking in a small
Florida town / Erin C. Heil.
  Includes bibliographical references and index.
  ISBN 978-1-935049-51-7 (hc: alk. paper)
  1. Slave labor—Florida—Immokalee. 2. Human trafficking—Florida—Immokalee.
3. Illegal aliens—Florida—Immokalee. 4. Prostitution—Florida—Immokalee. I. Title.
  HD4865.U6.H45 2012
  331.11'7340975944—dc23   2012013548

British Cataloguing in Publication Data
A Cataloguing in Publication record for this book
is available from the British Library.

This book was produced from digital files prepared by the author
using the FirstForumComposer.

Printed and bound in the United States of America

⊗   The paper used in this publication meets the requirements
    of the American National Standard for Permanence of
    Paper for Printed Library Materials Z39.48-1992.

5 4 3 2 1

Contents

Tables

Acknowledgments

I would like to acknowledge, first and foremost, the legal professionals and advocates who assisted me with my research. Without the information they provided, this book would not have been possible. Their battle against human trafficking of course goes far beyond this book, and I am humbled that they let me tell their stories.

We must remember that beyond the victims represented on the pages that follow there are thousands more—more than we can know—who continue to be trafficked into the United States and forced into slavery. Despite our awareness, the problem persists.

Additionally, I would like to thank all of the friends I made during my travels to Immokalee and the surrounding communities. I am particularly grateful to the proprietor of the Dolphin Inn, who always provided my accommodations while I was in Florida, and who through our conversations also became a supporter of my research and this book.

I would like to thank Andrew Berzanskis, who came to me with an idea and assisted every step of the way as it developed into a book.

My work would be impossible without friends and family with whom I am constantly developing my ideas, and I am fortunate to have so many patient and considerate people in my life. I am very grateful to all of them for their support of this project over the past three years. Last, but not least, I would like to thank my husband, Aaron, for supporting me and pushing me to keep writing. He always has believed in me, and I thank him with all of my heart.

1

The Problem of Forced Labor

*"Neither slavery nor involuntary servitude...shall exist within the
United States, or any place subject to their jurisdiction."*
—13th Amendment, U.S. Constitution

On January 17, 2007, nine family members were charged with forcing
undocumented immigrants to work in slave-like conditions in
Immokalee, Florida. Two family members, Cesar Navarrete and
Geovanni Navarrete, in addition to seven other defendants, were charged
with "beat[ing], threaten[ing], restrain[ing] and lock[ing] workers in
trucks to force them to work for them as agricultural laborers" (United
States Department of Justice, January 17, 2008, usdoj.gov). According
to local advocates and detectives, the agricultural workers had been
locked in a boxcar every night for a number of years. The boxcar had no
facilities, forcing the workers to sleep in the same corners where they
had to urinate and defecate. The doors to the boxcar remained locked
while the Florida sun beat down on its top, causing the temperatures
inside to spike over one hundred degrees, with relatively no ventilation.
Because of their addiction to alcohol, the workers would remain
compliant to their situation, the slavers found, if they were given a jug of
malt liquor in the morning and one at night.

In addition to the subhuman living conditions, the slavers also
charged outrageous fees for any food or facilities that the workers might
need so that they would be able to work for approximately ten hours in
the fields the following day. For example, the slavers would charge the
workers fifteen dollars so that they could shower with a garden hose.
Outrageous fees for everyday commodities such as food and water
perpetuated the slave's debt, so that he would never be able to work his
way out of his confinement. Years passed as the slaves accrued more
debt with no relief in sight.

There was no possibility of escape for the worker, and even if he did escape, he has been told a number of stories that restrained him psychologically to that boxcar. First, he understands that if he were to report himself to the authorities, he would be deported. He has been told that, because he is here illegally, the authorities will not listen to, nor will they believe, his reports of slavery. Second, he believes that everything that he has experienced will be all for naught. He has left his family, labored in the most inhumane conditions, and experienced an unimaginable life. He fears that his suffering will result in deportation, forcing him to begin the treacherous journey from the beginning with nothing to show for his suffering. Lastly, he fears retribution from his slaver if he is caught in an attempt to escape. The reality is that no one knows where he is. Who would know if he simply disappeared? And this is the power of the slaver, for he is fully aware that the people he is keeping in captivity are entirely disposable and replaceable. That is why the slaves in this case never tried to escape.

Despite the fears of escaping and reporting the slavery, one worker took a remarkable risk and was able to escape his captivity. Discovering a vulnerable area of the wall of the boxcar, he was able to force his way to freedom and report on the others who remained behind. Based on the evidence brought forth to legal officials by the workers, Cesar and Geovanni Navarrete were charged with slavery, and each faced up to two hundred years in federal prison for the enslavement of the workers. In September 2008, five of the nine defendants plead guilty to "harboring undocumented foreign nationals for private financial gain and identity theft," as well as "beating, threatening, restraining, and locking workers in trucks" (United States Department of State, September 3, 2008, usdoj.gov). Cesar and Geovanni each received twelve years in federal prison for the crime of enslaving undocumented workers.

During the time the laborers were attempting to escape their enslavement, a young girl was coming to the United States in search of a better life for herself. At the age of twelve, Daniela, who was living in Mexico, was approached by an older woman who offered her a job as a nanny in the United States.[1] As Daniela conveyed to local officials and advocates, who then told the story to me, the woman concocted a believable story of a family for whom she had been working for a number of years. Unfortunately, circumstances beyond her control had forced her to return to Mexico. The woman explained to Daniela that before she left the United States, she had promised the family that she would find an adequate replacement to continue her domestic responsibilities. She promised Daniela that she would be well paid and that the family would help her earn her citizenship, as well as providing her with food, housing, clothing, and education. This was the Daniela's chance for a new life full of promise and opportunity.

Arrangements were made to smuggle the Daniela into the United States; she would be met by a woman in Immokalee, Florida, who would act as a liaison to the family that would hire her. As promised, Daniela was met by a friendly woman who offered to let Daniela stay with her in Immokalee until the family could make arrangements for her to be taken to her new home and begin her domestic responsibilities. Unbeknownst to the young child as she trustingly followed the woman home, her nightmare had just begun.

Upon arrival to the home in Immokalee, the woman immediately began grooming Daniela for prostitution. She warned Daniela that if she tried to leave, she would be forced to pay thousands of dollars toward the debt she had accrued in her travels. She also threatened Daniela's family, and she reminded her that she was in the United States illegally and if she attempted to go to the police, she would be deported. Through the insurmountable debt and underlying fears, the woman was able to confine Daniela to a life of prostitution without the use of chains. In fact, she was so able to control Daniela through fear and intimidation that she allowed the young girl to leave the home on Sundays to attend church without a chaperone.

Despite the persistent threats, Daniela unearthed enough courage one Sunday to approach a man that she had previously befriended at church. She told him of her situation, and he promised to free her from her debt. He also told her that she would live with him and his family working as a domestic, and in return he would provide her with food, shelter, clothing, and education. To Daniela, this was the dream with which she initiated her journey to the United States. She allowed the man to speak with her "owner." The man made arrangements to pay Daniela's debt; in reality, he was purchasing Daniela from the woman. Once he had bought Daniela, he took her home, chained her to a basement wall, and repeatedly raped her. He continued to impregnate her, terminating any pregnancies in which the fetus was identified as female. He wanted a son, and so he continued to rape her until she bore him a boy. At the age of sixteen, through the communication and awareness of the local police and unfaltering advocates, as well as concerned neighbors and medical professionals, Daniela and her baby boy were identified and freed. She was granted a T-Visa, enrolled in high school, and began the life for which she had hoped when she began her journey to the United States. The "owner" and his wife were arrested for Daniela's enslavement and sexual assaults, and at the time of this writing, the trial is still pending.

Most readers have likely heard horrific stories of forced labor and are somewhat aware of its existence in the United States. Just as when I approached the topic myself, most readers may find the topic interesting, and find the testimonies of victims compelling. Workers being held in crowded rooms without electricity, young girls forced into prostitution to pay off a debt—these are the stories that readers are most likely to come across. Whether it is a national sporting event that raises awareness of the possibility of domestic trafficking, or the identification and prosecution of a major trafficking ring, the sporadic attention of the media leads many to believe that modern-day slavery is an extreme activity that occurs on the fringe of society. However, the stories that we read and hear barely scratch the surface of the enormity of slavery today. Many of the voices remain muted, as the slaves are hidden from the public eye. There are individuals, however, who are able to give a voice to the voiceless: the advocates and legal professionals in the local community. These individuals form the front line of fighters in the war against modern-day slavery. After years of working with and talking to these professionals, I decided to write a book revealing the anti-trafficking efforts of those at the local level and the obstacles they face as they attempt to eradicate trafficking and forced labor in their own community. This book is a case study of one small town in the United States where sexual slavery, forced agricultural labor, and domestic servitude have all been identified. This small town is Immokalee, Florida.

Immokalee, Florida, as a Case Study

I chose to write this case study on Immokalee because the town is in many ways a microcosm of human trafficking. In the United States, human trafficking takes various forms, including trafficking for purposes of domestic servitude, prostitution, servile marriage, factory work, begging/peddling, agriculture, restaurant work, and construction work. Research (e.g., United Nations, 2009) indicates that, both worldwide and in the United States, forced sexual exploitation and forced labor are the two most common forms of human trafficking identified by legal personnel and advocates. Trafficking for purposes of sexual exploitation overlaps with domestic servitude, for many of those who are forced to partake in domestic responsibilities also are sexually exploited. Therefore, throughout the United States, the main forms of human trafficking that have been identified are sexual in nature, or forced labor for little to no pay. In Immokalee, a town no larger than eight square miles, sexual slavery, agricultural slavery, and domestic servitude have all been identified. Because of the concentration of slave cases that have been detected in Immokalee, federal prosecutor Doug Molloy has dubbed the town "ground-zero" for modern-day slavery, while others have deemed it the "gate of no return" (Holt-Giménez 2009).

In addition to the types of slavery evident in Immokalee, the profiles of the trafficked victims and the traffickers, as well as how the victims are recruited, are illustrative of the patterns identified in communities throughout the United States. Although it is possible for victims of trafficking to be U.S. citizens, those identified have been found more likely to be noncitizens. There is no sex favoritism in trafficking; identified victims have been both men and women, although female victims trafficked for purposes of sexual exploitation tend to receive more media coverage. Victims can be any age, with some as young as three years old while others are in their sixties and seventies. Substantiating the profile of human trafficking victims, those identified in Immokalee are largely noncitizens; both men and women are victims, with ages varying from eight years to the late sixties. Although victim country of origin may differ in communities throughout the United States (i.e., victims of Asian, Eastern European, or African origin versus the concentration of Mexican and Central American victims in Immokalee), the victim profile in Immokalee corresponds with the general trend evident in communities throughout the United States.

Finally, the traffickers and the methods of recruitment found in Immokalee are representative of the patterns recognized throughout the United States. Of those who have been identified, the recruiting traffickers may be neighbors, friends, family members, returnees, agricultural operators, business owners, and organized criminals. Traffickers recruit victims through a variety of means including: newspaper ads, front businesses, word of mouth, and abduction. As in the story of the enslaved workers and of Daniela highlighted above, trafficking victims in Immokalee are recruited through similar means, by traffickers who fit the profile of those found in all corners of the United States. Regardless of location, the motive of the trafficker remains the same: traffickers prey on the vulnerable in order to earn a profit through the labor of a select few whom they regard as a disposable population.

It is because of these profiles, types, and trafficking indicators that I have chosen to write a case study of Immokalee. This case study could have been any community in the United States, for human trafficking is evident throughout the country, both in large cities and small towns.

However, I found Immokalee to be unique in that it is so hidden in the vast landscape of southern Florida, so lost in everyday conversation, that I felt it necessary to not only expand the discussion of the slavery evident in Immokalee, but also to provide a voice for the advocates for the victims, to aid their attempts to eradicate human trafficking in this small agricultural community.

About Immokalee, Florida

The first time I traveled to Immokalee, I was taken aback by the stunning contrast as I drove forty minutes outside of affluent Naples to find myself in a town comparable to the impoverished South American communities I have studied previously. Just a few blocks beyond the Seminole Casino, I observed small cubicle buildings with the word "BAR" painted over the entrance, unpaved side roads leading to trailers and shacks, and numerous people wandering the streets or sitting on their porches just to find relief from their sweltering homes. I was fascinated by the wild chickens and stray dogs that had commandeered the streets as I drove the back roads. My mind could not wrap itself around this community's presence in the back yard of the manicured aesthetic of one of the wealthiest cities in all of Florida.

I step out of my car, attempting to capture my breath in the suffocating heat. The town appears calm, almost completely silent beyond the sounds of squeaking bicycle brakes or the hum of a car slowly motoring through town. My first stop is the Immokalee police substation, but there is plenty of time before my scheduled meeting with local officers, so I decide to walk around the small block to see what I can discover. Across the street is a large single-story yellow building, which I later learn is the headquarters for the Coalition of Immokalee Workers. As I turn the corner to walk past the front of the building, two men sitting on the concrete porch eye me curiously. I walk past them, feeling their eyes fixated on me. Soon I will learn that, due to the exclusivity of the migrant community, strangers are easily identified. I smile at them, to which they respond in kind, and I continue around the building back to the main street. Although I have been out of the comfort of my air-conditioned car for no more than a few minutes, I can already feel the sun burning the back of my neck and sweat forming on my brow. The heat is exhausting, and I search the horizon for any indication of a familiar grocery store or convenience mart so that I can buy a bottle of water.

Continuing on the road that brought me into Immokalee, I walk past a number of housing units. To my right is a subcommunity of small white concrete homes with makeshift curtains blowing through the cutout windows in the concrete walls. There appear to be about a dozen of these homes, all the same size and model. The houses form a semicircle around a mountain of trash. The smell of the trash in the midday heat is overwhelming, and it attracts a population of flies and stray dogs searching for scraps. Above this tableau, buzzards continuously circle. The homes appear to be deserted at this time of day, with maybe one or two stragglers sitting on their front stoop. I later learn that I have stumbled upon one of the rental communities owned by a tomato grower, with migrant field workers as tenants.

Reminiscent of historic company towns, many of these subcommunities are scattered throughout Immokalee. Some seem to be semi-organized, like this group of white block homes or the apartment complexes located across the street. Some migrant housing is in trailer parks, while other migrant workers find housing in shacks or large garden sheds. Whatever type of housing, it is apparent that each community is segregated by country of origin—Mexicans, Haitians, and Guatemalans all living within the comfort of their own culture. Following the trend of segregation, there are also stores that cater to the various ethnic groups residing in the migrant communities. Across the street from the apartment complex identified as the Haitian community is a store that carries predominantly Haitian products. Farther down the road is a store that carries goods, such as distinctive spices and religious candles, more likely to appeal to members of the communities of Central-American descent.

Within a three-block range, I find a pinhooking market, where fresh produce, the leftovers of the daily harvest picked by the migrant workers, is sold to members of the local and neighboring communities for absurdly low prices; I am told this is a weekend destination for the Naples elite. There are also a number of independent cultural markets and a handful of bars. Occasionally, one may see a vendor standing on the corners selling *elote* (grilled Mexican corn on the cob covered in mayonnaise) from a street cart. There are a few restaurants in this center part of the town, and overall, everything seems to cater to short-term consumption rather than organized storage of the everyday needed goods. Even the small Immokalee motel has a reputation as charging by the hour, rather than by the day.

There are bicycles everywhere. In fact, in this small area where I find myself wandering, the number of bikes surpasses the number of automobiles. Ironically, there is absolutely no sign of a bicycle repair shop, or even a shop that sells bicycles. It leaves me to wonder where all the bikes came from, and more importantly, where bicycle owners go if a bike is in need of repair. The bicycles are just another indication of the mobile life of the migrant workers residing in Immokalee during the months of October through May. I stand on the sidewalk outside the Immokalee substation taking in the whole of parts though which I have just wandered. The world seems quiet and simple, yet hidden beneath the quiet solitude of the midweek afternoon, the reality is that the invisible residents are toiling in the midday heat, hoping to earn enough for a beer and snack after a long day of intense labor. I walk toward the substation to find the relief of air-conditioned comfort and to meet my first contact.

After my interview with the local police, I decide to explore the town beyond a few blocks of diameter. Surprisingly, as I drive down the main street the town opens up into a more recognizable "small town USA." There are the requisite McDonald's, grocery store, and bank. I drive to Lake Trafford to watch the alligators as they nap in the afternoon sun. A number of men sit lazily by the lake with fishing poles in hands. Beyond the "nucleus" of migrant activity, the area of Immokalee resembles so many other small towns scattered throughout the United States. It is unassuming for the outsider who happens to stumble upon this section of the town. There is no distinguishing feature to indicate that this small town is a hub of sex trafficking and forced labor. It is quiet and uneventful, as small middle-class homes populate this side of the Immokalee landscape and familiar restaurant chains and stores fill the mini-malls. I see the children exiting the small school and realize that it is time for me to return to what I have deemed to be the center of activity for my research: the block and corresponding side streets of First and Main. In this small area are the Coalition of Immokalee Workers headquarters, the police substation, and a large percentage of the already identified worker housing and later-to-be-found hidden brothels.

In the years following that initial visit, I have continued to return to the "center" of the town, always observing a virtually unchanged scene. And as I continued to dig deeper into the phenomena of modern slavery, I could not help but find a warm place in my heart for all of those affected by trafficking and all of those on the front line attempting to eradicate it. For each year I return to Immokalee, I now know why Immokalee has become a semi-permanent home for those migrant workers who continue to return each year, and for the advocates and local police who have chosen Immokalee as home. It is a town of familiarity and comfort, lost in the vast Florida terrain. Despite the horrific conditions associated with the agricultural labor and forced sex, the inhabitants of Immokalee attempted to maintain the meaning of the word Immokalee: "My Home."

Definitional Issues

Forced labor is a product of human trafficking and labor migration. Although the term "human trafficking" is freely applied, both historically and internationally, there has not always been an agreed upon definition of the term. As stated by Clawson et al., "prior to the 1990s, trafficking was generally viewed as a form of human smuggling and a type of illegal migration" (2006: 9). Today, it remains understood that there is much "overlap between trafficking, smuggling and other forms of irregular migration...and they share many of the same root causes" (Turner and Kelly 2009: 187). As identified by Turner and Kelly:

> Wars, conflicts, and the social and economic crises generated in some regions of the world...the destabilizing effects of globalization and transition have contributed to large and irregular population flows, creating 'fertile fields for exploitation' (ibid.: 187)

Despite the similar root causes, smuggling, migration, and trafficking are uniquely distinct. According to U.S. Immigration and Customs Enforcement, "human smuggling is the importation of people into a country via the deliberate evasion of immigration laws. This offense includes bringing illegal aliens into a country, as well as the unlawful transportation and harboring of aliens already in a country illegally" (ICE.gov 2010, accessed May 2010). Migration, on the other hand, is defined as "having traveled at least 75 miles within the previous year to obtain a farm job" (National Center for Farmworker and Health, Inc., 2009). Individuals who have been smuggled into the United States or those who migrate across domestic and/or national borders are free to move from location to location, as well as free to switch occupations. There is a voluntary nature inherent in smuggling and migration that makes these form of movements unique from trafficking.

Trafficking in persons is identified in the Protocol to Prevent, Suppress, and Punish Trafficking in Persons, Especially Women and Children, Supplementing the United Nations Convention against Transnational Crime (2000). According to the Protocol,

> 'Trafficking in persons' shall mean the recruitment, transportation, transfer, harbouring or receipt of persons, by means of the threat or use

of force or other forms of coercion, of abduction, of fraud, of deception, of the abuse of power or of a position of vulnerability or of the giving or receiving of payments or benefits to achieve the consent of a person having control over another person, for the purpose of exploitation. Exploitation shall include, at a minimum, the exploitation of the prostitution of others or other forms of sexual exploitation, forced labour or services, slavery or practices similar to slavery, [or] servitude... (United Nations 2000: Article 3)

The central component that separates trafficking from smuggling and migration is coercion. With trafficking, a person is coerced and forced to work in a system of slavery or experience slave-like work conditions. It is very possible, though, that a person who has been smuggled or who migrates will become a victim of trafficking. This occurs when the smuggler or employer makes the decision to benefit from the exploitation of services, and the once voluntary movement becomes one of domineering control. In other words, if the victim is subjected to forced labor, the individual is now trafficked and the movement and work are no longer voluntary.

The International Labour Organization (ILO) Convention No. 29 (1930) defines forced labor as "all work or service which is exacted from any person under the menace of any penalty and for which the said person has not offered himself voluntarily" (Article 2.1). The two criteria of forced labor are the "menace of the penalty and the 'involuntariness'" (Belser 2005: 3). Some workers may consent to work, but the "consent of workers is irrelevant when there has been deception or fraud, or the retention of identity documents in order to achieve this consent" (ibid.: 3). In other words, the consent of a worker is void if it is a product of fraud or deception. Once there is consent to work, menace of penalty may come in the form of "physical violence or death threats...the denunciation to the police...when the victim's residence or work status is illegal, [or] the confiscation of work papers..." (ibid.: 3). Thus, it is very common for a migrant or smuggled person to enter into a situation of forced labor under false pretenses. On the other hand, due to the inherent involuntariness, the majority of human trafficking cases in the world take the form of forced labor.

In terms of voluntariness, the age of the victim is critical to consent. Children under the age of eighteen found performing commercial sex acts will automatically be defined as victims of trafficking, being unable to legally provide consent. On the other hand, the federal legislation does not automatically identify children under the age of eighteen laboring in the fields, domestically, or in factories as victims of trafficking. Therefore, in order to identify a victim of labor trafficking, a child under the age of eighteen has the same responsibility as an individual over eighteen to prove that the labor is a product of force, fraud, or coercion. Thus, when weeding out the victims of trafficking from those who voluntarily choose to illegally enter the United States or migrate across borders during the various harvest seasons, age of consent is only valid for those found in the commercial sex industry.

According to a local detective who I interviewed, without giving exact numbers, he believed that the majority of immigrants living and working in Immokalee had been trafficked into the area in some way, while a smaller percentage have been smuggled or migrate to the area each harvest season. Despite the type of movement, the prime concern of this book is the system of slavery in which men, women, and children are forced to work once they find themselves in Immokalee. In this community, two primary forms of forced labor have been identified.[2] The first of these is forced commercial sexual acts, which includes "women, men and children who have been forced by private agents into prostitution or into other forms of commercial sexual activities" (ibid.: 3). The other type is forced labor for economic exploitation, which includes "all forced labor imposed by private agents and enterprises in sectors other than the sex industry. It includes all forced labour [sic] in agriculture, industry, and services..." (ibid.: 3). Commercial sexual exploitation and economic exploitation are not exclusive to Immokalee, for forced labor has been identified in at least ninety cities in the United States and in virtually every country worldwide.

Forced Labor Worldwide

Due to the covert nature of the crime, any statistical estimate concerning forced labor must be approached with caution. Currently, the ILO estimates that 12.3 million people worldwide work in conditions of forced labor, slavery, and slave-like conditions (International Labour Organization, 2009). This estimate includes women and children forced into prostitution and other forms of sexual exploitation, individuals trapped in debt bondage, and individuals forced into sweatshops and agricultural work for little or no pay. Of the 12.3 million, "the ILO found that almost 2.5 million people who are exploited by private agents and enterprises are in forced labour [sic] as a result of human trafficking" (Belser: 5). Of the 2.5 million trafficked laborers, the ILO estimates "that at least 1.39 million are victims of commercial sexual servitude, both transnational and within countries" (Department of State 2009: 3), and another "1.1 million in...economic exploitation" (Belser: 5). As highlighted in the Trafficking in Persons Report (TIP) (2010), "the ILO estimates that for every trafficking victim subjected to forced prostitution, nine people are forced to work" (8).

Forced labor exists in virtually every corner of the world. For example, in Malaysia, migrants travel from nearby countries and are

> subsequently subjected to conditions of involuntary servitude in the domestic, agricultural, food service, construction, plantation, industrial, and fisheries sectors. Some foreign women and girls are also victims of commercial sexual exploitation. Some migrant workers are victimized by their employers, employment agents, or traffickers who supply migrant laborers and victims of sex trafficking. Some victims suffer conditions including physical and sexual abuse, forced drug use, debt bondage, non-payment of wages, threats, confinement, and withholding of travel documents to restrict their freedom of movement (Department of State TIP 2009: 197).

In Brazil, agricultural workers, many of whom have been replaced by machinery, consent to loans for travel to a promised employment— loans that are impossible to repay. Once workers reach their destination, they have to begin repaying the loan, as well as pay for rent, food, and equipment. If the workers attempt to leave without repaying the dept, they will be captured and returned to the worksite or murdered. "In a study of 475 labor case of the 1990s, '20.7% of all forced labourers had been killed'" (Comissão Pastoral da Terra, quoted in Heil 2008: 73). Aside from the threat of death and overbearing debt, workers have been faced with "sleeping in chicken houses, food consisting of dead rats, flooding of shacks, and malaria infections. As for the actual work, laborers suffer from smoke inhalation, mutilation, dehydration, and heat exhaustion" (ibid.).

In Africa, the trafficking of children is spurred by poverty, conflict, and cultural traditions. As reported by Fleck, children as young as eight years of age are sold as prostitutes or laborers, and many are recruited as child soldiers (2004).

> Children from war ravaged West African countries [are] often sold as slave labourers to work on tea, cotton, and cocoa plantations. Girls from Togo [are] trafficked far from home as domestic servants. In Malawi, European tourists drive demand for child prostitutes, and some of those children are sent to Europe as sex slaves (ibid.: 1).

According to the United Nations, "human trafficking flows show that Europe is affected in three ways: most of Europe is a destination for victims of trafficking, some countries are significant origins of human trafficking, and domestic trafficking is prevalent in many countries" (United Nations 2009: 10). Europe is unique in that the victims of trafficking and forced labor come from the most diverse origin countries. Victims originate from Romania, Paraguay, Nigeria, the Russian Federation, and many more. The majority of the victims are adult women forced into commercial sexual exploitation, but there has been an emergence of adult men being forced into the construction and agricultural sectors, among other forms of economic exploitation. Research on Europe has revealed that children are rarely identified as victims of forced labor (sexual or economic). In 2008, children comprised of only 11 percent of the identified victims (ibid.).

Because of the allure of an economy overflowing with opportunity, the United States is regarded as a central destination country for many victims of human trafficking. As with international estimates, the number of individuals trafficked across and within borders varies. As Lendman noted (2009), "[there are] thousands annually trafficked in America in over 90 cities; around 17,000 by some estimates and up to 50,000 according to the CIA..." (www.globalresearch.ca, accessed July 2009). According to a 2004 UC Berkeley study, "forced labor is prevalent in five sectors of the U.S. economy: prostitution and sex services (46 percent), domestic service (27 percent), agriculture (10 percent), sweatshop/factory (5 percent) and restaurant and hotel work (4 percent)" (University of California, Berkeley: 1). Unfortunately, "estimates on the number of persons being trafficked often only include data on women and children who are being sexually exploited" (Clawson et al. 2006: 8), thereby skewing the reality of trafficking. Recent worldwide field studies have concluded that the demand for forced labor is much higher than estimated, making labor trafficking more widespread than sex trafficking (Feingold 2005).

In 2010, for the first time, the United States was examined in the Department of State's annual Trafficking in Persons (TIP) Report. Since 2000, TIP has been an annual report card for countries throughout the globe, placing each country on a tier in terms of its attempts to eradicate internal human trafficking and forced labor. The United States has been ranked as a Tier One country, which means that it fully complies with the minimum standards of anti-trafficking efforts. Despite U.S. efforts, however, it has been reported that

> [t]rafficking occurs primarily for labor and most commonly in domestic servitude, agriculture, manufacturing, janitorial services, hotel services, construction, health and elder care, hair and nail salons, and strip club dancing. Vulnerabilities remain even for legally

documented temporary workers who typically fill labor needs in the hospitality, landscaping, construction, food service, and agricultural industries. In some human trafficking cases, workers are victims of fraudulent recruitment practices and have incurred large debts for promised employment in the United States, which makes them susceptible to debt bondage and involuntary servitude. Trafficking cases also involve passport confiscation, nonpayment or limited payment of wages, restriction of movement, isolation from the community, and physical and sexual abuse as means of keeping victims in compelled service (2010: 338).

Table 1.1: Known Trafficking Victims Identified by State[3]

State	Percent of Known Victims
Texas	12%
California	10%
Florida	4%
New York	4%
District of Columbia	4%

National Human Trafficking Resource Center (2009)

As Table 1.1 indicates, some areas are known hot-spot destinations for human trafficking. For example, in 2008, 12 percent of victims of human trafficking were identified in Texas, whereas another 10 percent of victims were identified in California. Despite the hot-spot destinations, research has revealed that most states have some form of forced labor. In fact, according to the U.S. Department of Justice, there are currently open human trafficking investigations in forty-eight states. For example, North Carolina is one of the top agricultural states in the country and ranks fifth in migrant population; most of these migrants are from Mexico. Although a large percentage of the workers are migrants consenting to work, they are still considered forced laborers because of fraudulent promises and menace of penalty. Once a commitment has been made to work in the fields, workers labor long days in intense heat with limited breaks. Many of the fields lack toilets and sanitary facilities, and a large number of workers have been exposed to agricultural illnesses such as green tobacco poisoning and/or pesticide sickness (see Legal Aid of North Carolina 2010).

Not all of the laborers in North Carolina are Mexican migrants who have accepted jobs under false promises of pay and standard work conditions. Recently, a trend has been to recruit workers from Asia. The organization Legal Aid of North Carolina reports "at least 115 workers whom contractors brought to North Carolina from the Far East between 2004 and 2006" (humantrafficking.org, accessed July 2010). Once the workers have moved to the United States, their money is stolen, they are not paid, and they are held captive with threats of violence. According to one case, the defendants had their passports confiscated and were forced to work with no pay. They had their food rationed, and they resorted to capturing pigeons for food. While living in a condemned hotel, they were able to escape and bring the atrocities of their servitude to the attention of the legal authorities (*Asanok et al. v. Million Express Manpower, Inc.,* 2007).

Between 2003 and 2005, Aloun Farms of Hawaii enslaved 44 Thai workers. According to Kloer, "the recruiters charged each of the workers $16,000 to bring them to the U.S. and find them work at Aloun Farms. Once in Hawaii, the workers were told they must pay off this debt before receiving a paycheck" (Kloer 2010: 1). Most of the workers were unable to pay the debt, and therefore never received a paycheck for their labor. In addition to the lack of pay, workers were threatened with deportation, and were not allowed to communicate with anyone outside of the laboring community. In 2010 the company president and his brother pleaded guilty to forced labor charges, and as of this writing, the punishment is still pending (ibid.).

California is estimated to be one of the top three destination locations of human trafficking in the United States. "The state's extensive international border, its major harbors and airports, its powerful economy and accelerating population, its large immigrant population and its industries make it a prime target for traffickers" (California Alliance to Combat Trafficking and Slavery Task Force 2007: 15). The cases of trafficking and forced labor throughout the state are diverse. Women have been forced to work in exotic massage parlors, young girls have been enslaved as domestic servants, and men have been forced to work in the construction industry with little to no pay. Migrants have been forced to labor in fields under the harshest of conditions, and workers have been found imprisoned within the walls of garment factories. Young girls have also been found in brothels and prostitution rings throughout the state (ibid.).

The Midwest has not always been regarded as a hub of human trafficking, but evidence indicates that a growing number of trafficked individuals are forced into sexual slavery there. For example, according to the Department of Homeland Security in Illinois, "an estimated minimum of 16,000 to 25,000 women and girls are victims of commercial sexual exploitation in Chicago every year" (Department of Homeland Security Illinois 2010). With respect to trafficking, "from December 2007 to June 2009, 257 calls were made from Illinois to the National Human Trafficking Resource Center. This is the fifth highest number of calls after Texas, California, New York, and Florida" (ibid). Trafficked victims in Kansas City, Missouri, have been rescued from massage parlors on two separate occasions, which leads many to believe that the trend is continuing to grow in the Kansas City area (see *Kansas City Business Journal*, August 21, 2008; *Kansas City Star*, May 11, 2007). Additionally, an undercover investigation called "Operation Guardian Angels" exposed child prostitution rings in the Kansas City and surrounding communities (KNBC.com, accessed April 2010). In 2006, "Civil Society [a Minnesota nonprofit] had identified 24 immigrants brought to Minnesota for the purposes of sexual exploitation, forced labor, indentured servitude or 'mail order' sham marriages..." (Rosario 2006, www.wunrn.com, accessed April 2010). Civil Society also notes that "Minnesota has become one of the 13 most heavily sex and slavery trafficked states in the nation" (www.civilsocietyhelps.org, accessed April 2010). Recently, in Missouri, a man was indicted for harboring a young woman as a sex slave. She was electrocuted, flogged, mutilated, and raped by multiple men in exchange for various commodities, including steaks and cigarettes (St. Louis Today, March 31, 2011, www.stltoday.com, accessed, April, 2011)

As indicated by the above examples, trafficking and forced labor are prevalent throughout the United States. In response to the heightened awareness, the federal government and international bodies have enacted a number of laws to eliminate the practices of trafficking and slavery. The most prominent of these in use in the United States are the Protocol to Prevent, Suppress, and Punish Trafficking in Persons, Especially Women and Children (also known as the Palermo Protocol), the Trafficking in Persons Act of 2000, the Trafficking in Persons Reauthorization Act of 2008, and the United Nations International Convention on the Protection of the Rights of All Migrant Workers and Members of Their Families.

Laws Against Trafficking and Forced Labor

The Palermo Protocol, adopted by the United Nations, has identified what it calls the 3-Ps to combat human trafficking and forced labor:

criminal prosecution, victim protection, and prevention. The Palermo Protocol recognizes trafficking as an offense "akin to murder, rape, and kidnapping. Criminalization is mandatory for all parties to the Palermo Protocol, and the importance of prosecution is reflected in the U.S. law enforcement approach" (2010: 12–13). In other words, human trafficking and forced labor are not simple issues of immigration violation, but rather crimes that require written laws to interpret and punish the offense.

When it comes to victim protection, the Protocol takes a victim-centered approach. As noted by Rijken and Koster (2008), "the crime of trafficking is often approached from a criminal law perspective with the aim to catch the perpetrators. In this approach, attention for victims is practically only present to the extent they are relevant for law enforcement purposes" (1). Furthermore, "too often, governments respond to [trafficked human beings] as a migration problem rather than a human rights challenge, using trafficking as a justification for tighter border controls. This has led to the deportation of trafficking victims…without adequate consideration for their safety and well-being" (ibid.: 11). The Palermo Protocol insists that nation states should not assist "a potential witness just long enough to get his or her testimony" but rather meet the needs and fulfill obligations "that extend beyond the confines of a criminal case" (Department of State 2010; 13). States should cooperate with advocates and service providers to protect the interests of the victims throughout the prosecutorial process, as well as after the victim has assisted in the prosecution.

Traditionally, prevention had been understood as education, border security initiatives, and public awareness campaigns. Today, "governments are expanding their understanding of prevention to include policies and practices that cut off modern slavery at the source. This includes initiatives that both combat the demand for commercial sex and ensure that the demand for low prices is balanced by a demand for traceability, transparency, and worker protections throughout the supply chain" (ibid.: 14). Aside from identifying and attempting to eradicate the sources of modern slavery, the Protocol also insists that signatory countries recognize the various legal loopholes that foster a system of the criminalization and deportation of a vulnerable population, as well as provide adequate awareness of and assistance to the marginalized workers. Finally, according to the Protocol, "Prevention also can and should harness the economic impetus for this crime in order to fight it—by increasing criminal or civil penalties for companies that directly rely on forced labor in the production of goods or services" (ibid.: 15).

To address the pervasiveness of trafficking in the United States, the U.S. Congress passed the Trafficking Victim Protections Act (TVPA) in 2000, which provides the tools to combat human trafficking both domestically and internationally. The purpose of the law is to prevent trafficking, protect victims, and prosecute offenders. Specifically, the Act criminalizes trafficking and forced labor, provides for social services and benefits to victims of slavery and trafficking, provides protection for victims both in the United States and in the victims' countries of origin, and makes attempts to monitor and eliminate trafficking outside of the United States. The Act predominantly protects children who have been trafficked into the United States for the purpose of sex, but with respect to forced labor and slavery, the Act strengthens prosecutorial efforts and the punishment of offenders. According to the Act,

> Whoever knowingly provides or obtains the labor or services of a person (1) by threats of serious harm to, or physical restraint against, that person or another person; (2) by means of any scheme, plan, or pattern intended to cause the person to believe that, if the person did not perform such labor or services, that person or another person would suffer serious harm or physical restraint; or (3) by means of the abuse or threatened abuse of law or the legal process, shall be fined...or imprisoned not more than 20 years or both (§ 1589, Forced Labor 2000).

The Act also states that "whoever knowingly recruits, harbors, transports, provides, or obtains by any means, any person for labor...in violation of this chapter shall be fined...or imprisoned not more than 20 years, or both" (§ 1590). Trafficking with respect to peonage, slavery, involuntary servitude, or forced labor, 2000).

In evaluating international efforts against trafficking, the TVPA requires countries to be placed on one of three tiers regarding their level of trafficking and government action to combat trafficking.[4] Governments that fully comply with eliminating trafficking are placed in Tier 1. Governments that reach the minimum standards of compliance are placed on the second tier. Some countries are placed on the Tier 2 watch list (WL). Governments on the watch list are reaching the minimum standards of compliance, but there is an identifiably significant increase in victims of trafficking, yet efforts are not being made to address the increase in trafficked victims. Lastly, governments that are not making efforts to comply with the TVPA are placed on Tier 3. According to the Department of State's Trafficking in Persons Report (2009), "governments of countries on Tier 3 may be subject to certain sanctions, whereby the U.S. Government may withhold or withdraw non-humanitarian, non-trade-related foreign assistance." (13). Currently, 13 countries are ranked as Tier 3 and 55 countries are on the Tier 2 watch list (see Appendix A).

Although the Act has been a source of combating trafficking in the United States and worldwide, it still has considerable shortcomings. The most problematic aspect of the TVPA is the role of the victim as a witness for the state. As noted in the study conducted by the University of California, Berkeley, "the Act conditions immigration relief and social services on prosecutorial cooperation and thus creates the perception that survivors are primarily instruments of law enforcement rather than individuals who are, in and of themselves, deserving of protection and restoration of their human rights" (University of California, Berkeley, 2004: 2). In other words, in order for victims to benefit from the TVPA, they must first assist law enforcement in prosecuting the traffickers, unless they are a child under the age of eighteen working in the commercial sex industry. These children automatically receive benefits regardless of whether they choose to assist prosecution. However, for victims over eighteen, or those not working in the commercial sex industry, the requirement to assist the prosecution has proven to be problematic in that many victims fear the repercussions of the traffickers both to the victim and to the victim's family in the country of origin. Despite its shortcomings, the TVPA has been legally emulated by many countries worldwide.

The Trafficking Victims Protection Reauthorization Act (TVPRA) of 2008 extended the TVPA for another four years. The TVPRA also amended the TVPA to include the following:

> Creates new categories of crimes for the obstruction of justice in the investigation of trafficking cases;
>
> "Broadens the crime of sex trafficking by force, fraud, or coercion" (DOJ 2009: 3);
>
> Imposes criminal liability on corporations that knowingly and with intent fraudulently hire individuals from outside of the United States;
>
> Allows for the United States to prosecute acts of trafficking *outside* of the United States (if the offender is a resident of the United States); and
>
> Expands the crime of forced labor by providing that "force" is a means of violating the law (in addition to making threats of serious harm, using a scheme or plan, or abusing the law) (ibid.: 3).

As regards migrant labor, undocumented immigrants are "expressly excluded from the definition of 'migrant worker' in most relevant international instruments with the exception of the...UN International Convention on the Protection of the Rights of All Migrant Workers and Members of Their Families" (Cholewinski 1997: 4). The purpose of this Convention, known as the UN Migration Convention, is to protect the fundamental human rights of migrant workers. According to the Convention, "no migrant worker or member of his or her family shall be subjected to torture or to cruel, inhumane or degrading treatment or punishment" (Article 10, 1990). Furthermore, "no migrant worker or member of his or her family shall be held in slavery or servitude" and "no migrant worker or member of his or her family shall be required to perform forced or compulsory labor" (Article 11). Although the United Nations has guidelines in place to protect migrant workers, only state signatories are legally bound to the provisions of the Convention. Currently, fifty-seven states have signed and/or ratified the UN Migration Convention. The majority of the state signatories are the country of origin of the migrant workers. As of this writing, the United States has not signed the UN Migration Convention.

Although both national and international efforts are being made to reduce human trafficking, the practice continues to grow in the United States. As Farrell found in her national survey of human trafficking, "relatively few trafficking arrests or prosecutions have been made by law enforcement" (2009: 246). According to her findings, prosecutions and arrests are low for four main reasons. The first is that many local law enforcement agents view human trafficking as a federal problem, not a local one. Second, police might not inquire into the immigration status of victims, thereby overlooking an important indicator of trafficking. Third, victims are usually identified as violating laws associated with immigration. When asked about their status, the threat of possible deportation limits the cooperation on the part of trafficked victims. Finally, because of cultural fears of law enforcement, many victims of trafficking resist law enforcement intervention. Internationally, in 2009 there were 4,166 successful trafficking prosecutions, 335 of which were related to forced labor. Unfortunately, 62 countries have yet to convict a trafficker under laws in compliance with the Palermo Protocol, and 104 countries still do not have laws in place to prevent victims' deportation (Department of State 2010).

The lack, in the United States, of criminal prosecution, victim protection, and prevention of trafficking and forced labor begs the question of the level at which anti-trafficking efforts are effective. Nationally and internationally, the laws and protocols that have been written and signed recognize the problem of human trafficking and forced labor as a federal issue. However, the efforts made in Immokalee highlight the reality that the issue of human trafficking and modern slavery needs to be understood in the local context. Based on years of interviews and observations in Immokalee, this book has as its purpose identifying the various forms of slavery in the area, and the local efforts that are being made to prevent future instances of trafficking and protect victims beyond the prosecutorial stage.

Methodology

When I first began data collection for this project in 2008, the research was exploratory in nature and sought to address how District 8 of the Collier County Sheriff's Office (Immokalee, Florida) responded to undocumented immigrants in the local community. It was conducted as a means of prompting future research. However, the initial data collection introduced me to an inconceivable web of complexities surrounding modern-day slavery, as well as the external measures that have been taken by a number of players who work together to improve the life conditions of those forced to labor in slave-like conditions. Therefore, what began as an open-ended question evolved over the next two years to become a book that I hope will allow the reader to experience and appreciate the intricacies of illegal immigration and human trafficking so evident in Immokalee.

The information reported in this book was collected through two years of interviews and field observations, which I conducted at District 8 of the Collier County Sheriff's Office, located in Immokalee, Florida; the Collier County Division of Human Trafficking located in Naples, Florida; and the district attorney's office located in Ft. Myers, Florida. I also conducted phone interviews and person-to-person interviews with local advocates associated with the Human Trafficking Task Force and with advocates associated with the Ft. Myers division of Catholic Charities.

Regarding legal professionals, the interviews with the local law enforcement were conducted with various officers at the district office and also while partaking in "ride-alongs." Forty-five questionnaires regarding police perceptions of undocumented immigrants and the 287(g) program (described in Chapter 4) were mailed prior to a visit, and distributed to the officers via their departmental mail slots. On the subsequent visit, twenty questionnaires were retrieved, and follow-up questions were conducted. Multiple one-on-one interviews were conducted with the members of the Division of Human Trafficking, as well as email and phone follow-ups. I also was able to observe the life conditions of the slave laborers and sex workers while partaking in ride-alongs with the Division of Human Trafficking. Finally, person-to-person interviews, as well as follow-up phone and email conversations, took place at the district attorney's office. It should be noted that much of the information regarding attitudes toward and actions related to local undocumented workers came from the legal professionals with whom I spoke. Because Immokalee is such a small town, and identifiers can easily disrupt anonymity, many of the responses and stories that are presented throughout the book are vaguely referenced as told to me by "a legal professional" or some other indicator of the interviewee's role in the battle against trafficking.

As already stated, I conducted phone interviews and follow-up person-to-person interviews with advocates associated with the Human Trafficking Task Force and Catholic Charities. I made multiple attempts to interview members of the Coalition of Immokalee Workers, the leading advocacy group working for agricultural slave rights. However, these attempts met with no response from members of the Coalition, so the information derived regarding this organization was developed through secondary media sources (e.g., the *New York Times*, *Gourmet* magazine), published books (see Bowe 2007), and the Coalition's website (ciw-online.org).

Aside from the interviews and observations, I also conducted analyses on arrest data located on the sheriff department's website.[5] The analysis included cause for arrest, country of origin of arrestee, and employment status of arrestee. Demographics (e.g., gender and age) were also recorded. This data was collected in the months of November through April (the peak harvest time) and compared over two years. Taken together, the information reported in this book represents the use of various methodologies to report an accurate account of human trafficking and the efforts taken to improve the life conditions of those trapped in slavery in Immokalee, Florida.

Organization of this Book

Readers must be aware that this is not another book solely devoted to defining human trafficking and forced labor, providing a discussion of statistics, and offering possible solutions to the problem. Although this information will be presented throughout the chapters, these concepts are not the central theme of the book. My intention here is to provide a voice not only for the victims, but also for the advocates and legal actors. Beyond telling the story of the people of Immokalee, I will also examine the root causes as to why slavery continues persists in the United States and the world. Chapter 2 will initiate the discussion of slavery by providing an overview of the agricultural slavery evident in Immokalee, Florida. In particular, this chapter will discuss the day-to-day activities of the field laborers in the months of October through May. Human rights violations, such as unacceptable working, living, and economic conditions, will be examined, as well as an analysis as to why these violations continue to occur. The chapter will also provide a sociological analysis of the gender and racial profiles of those working in the fields. In Chapter 3 the discussion of trafficking will shift to commercial sexual exploitation, emphasizing the victims, the abuse, the health issues, and the economic conditions associated therewith. This chapter will also use the sociological lens to analyze sex work in general, explore issues of gender and cultural *machismo*, and identify the differences and overlap between prostitutes in Immokalee and sexual slavery.

Chapters 4 and 5 will turn the focus toward local efforts to identify and protect the victims of trafficking and prosecute the offenders. Chapter 4 is an overview of the unique role law enforcement plays in a predominantly illegal community. The local police work in a district that has an agreement with the federal government to enforce immigration law. This creates a contradiction in responsibility for those obligated with the role of immigration enforcer while at the same time needing to promote a sense of community. However, the local police are not the only actors evident in this negotiating pattern. Collier County also retains a detective and an advocate who make up the Division of Human Trafficking and who partake in credible efforts toward the eradication of trafficking. With the cooperation of the assistant US district attorney, the combined efforts of the Division of Human Trafficking and the local police in Immokalee have generated national attention in their innovative approach to maintaining a sense of protection and community while weeding out the criminal elements.

Chapter 5 covers those organizations that work actively to educate the public on slavery while assisting the victims. The most prominent organization in assisting the farmworkers is the Coalition of Immokalee Workers (CIW). This group is "a community-based organization of mainly Latino, Mayan Indian and Haitian immigrants working in low-wage jobs throughout the state of Florida" (CIW-online.org). In their words, they fight for "a fair wage for the work we do, more respect on the part of our bosses and the industries where we work, better and cheaper housing, stronger laws and stronger enforcement against those who would violate workers' rights, the right to organize on our jobs without fear of retaliation, and an end to indentured servitude in the fields" (ibid). In addition to the CIW, the Human Trafficking Task Force and Catholic Charities are also central advocates in the mission of trafficking eradication. The Human Trafficking Task Force is a group of individuals who tackle the difficult task of educating the public and law enforcement on how to identify victims of human trafficking. Catholic Charities assists victims and educates the community on the various issues associated with human trafficking. This is not an exclusive list of the actors active in combating trafficking in Immokalee, but it is illustrative of the efforts that are being made by the local community.

The book concludes with an overall analysis of the persistence of modern-day slavery in Immokalee, Florida. Specifically, I will stress that state complicity is an obstacle to anti-trafficking efforts, and that until invisible lines are exposed, the practice of slavery will continue in the United States. The concluding chapter highlights that consumerism, racism, sexism, and stances against illegal immigration are not excuses to allow the practice of slavery to persist. As Bowe noted (2007), "everybody is a somebody" (xxii), and regardless of status, everybody should be protected under the umbrella of human rights.

---

[1] Names have been changed to protect anonymity.

[2] The terms "slavery and "forced labor" will be used interchangeably throughout the book.

[3] Information derived from National Human Trafficking Resource Center (2009). Estimates are based on number of calls and emails received regarding potential victims of human trafficking.

[4] Tier placements are reported annually in the Trafficking in Persons Report.

[5] www.colliersheriff.org

2

Agricultural Slavery

*"Slavery is theft—theft of a life, theft of work,
theft of any property or produce…"*
—Kevin Bales

It is dusk, as the sun is beginning to set on a Friday evening in Immokalee. The workers have just stepped off of the work buses, each worker carrying a watermelon in hand. The officer sitting with me scoffs to himself: "Looks like they got paid in produce today." I turn to him with a look of surprise, to which he only responds with a shrug of his shoulders. It is quite possible that these workers were paid with produce rather than cash. They have just worked over ten hours under the sun of a blistering 85-degree day with little to no break, and all they have to show for their work is one watermelon. No worker bothers to complain, for that would only result in termination from work, financial losses, and/or physical and psychological violence. Therefore, each worker hangs his head as he steps off the bus, cradling a watermelon in his arms. I have yet to see what sort of labor has led to the payment of watermelon, but now that the workers are safely back home, the officer decides to take me out to a tomato field.

After ten minutes or so on the road that exits from Immokalee, we turn onto a twisting road that alternates between asphalt and dirt. As we drive deeper and deeper into the backlands of the southern Florida landscape, walls of trees block any indication of a tomato field. Finally we turn into a driveway that opens up to miles of tomato plants. I stand in complete awe as the field seems to stretch into forever. It is early November, and the plants have not yet reached their full maturity. I ask the officer what would be the workers' responsibilities if there were no tomatoes to be picked at this time. I was told that each worker had the responsibility to cover the roots of the small plants to protect them from any sudden changes in the weather. To clarify, each plant was approximately two to three feet in height at this time. What this duty entailed was that each worker, for approximately ten hours in stagnant heat, had to take black garbage bags, cut an "X" in each one, and then gently place the covering over the plant so that the roots stay warm and safe from the elements. At the same time, the workers must also be sure not to disrupt the foliage and possible flowering buds on each tomato plant, for a damaged plant could incur a financial loss and possible physical abuse. The entire day, the workers had to stand in a bent-over position as they placed each of these coverings over immature tomato plants that grew over what seemed to be miles of fields. At end of all this painful and menial labor, each laborer stepped off of the labor bus with a watermelon. Another day without pay, another worker exploited, another farmer profiting, and another moment of misery—all have gone unnoticed as most of us begin another unassuming weekend in the month of November.

Horrific are the general living and working conditions of those trapped in agricultural slavery. The purpose of this chapter is not to sensationalize the gruesome details associated with forced labor, but rather to examine the conditions of forced agricultural labor, and to discuss the generalizable similarities of life conditions as well as the intricate distinctions associated with the migrant laborers caught in the same cycle of slavery. This chapter will be divided into several sections that together will develop a clear picture of the slavery associated with the tomato industry in Immokalee, Florida. I will begin by briefly discussing the key differences between traditional forms of slavery in comparison to modern slavery, after which I will provide a brief description of the invisibility of agriculture labor in Immokalee. This will be followed by an examination of the general similarities of agricultural slave laborers based on demographics such as sex, ethnicity, and age. The demographics of the workers are directly associated with the system of protection that is related to external support, and therefore I will examine how economic and political power is constructed based on legal and advocate-based systems of external support.

Following the general analysis of agricultural workers in Immokalee, I will narrow the discussion to the typical workday for those trapped in agricultural slavery. This will be followed by the identification of the general restraints that hold the workers in perpetual slavery. The chapter will conclude with an analysis as to why agricultural slavery persists in the twenty-first century in the United States and what can be learned from the Immokalee example. Although this chapter is specific to Immokalee, the patterns that emerge in this examination are evident in various forms of agricultural slavery in the country. The importance of this chapter is to utilize the information derived from Immokalee to specify those various characteristics that are generalizable to agricultural slavery throughout the United States. Immokalee serves as a unique case in that the slavery is confined to the desolate backfields of southern Florida, virtually invisible to the large majority of U.S. citizens. However, the characteristics of agricultural slavery in Immokalee are comparable to slavery across the agricultural landscape, and can serve as a stepping stone to understanding the life and work conditions, as well as the systems of relative power, associated with migrant labor and agricultural slavery. But before those characteristics may be addressed, it must first be determined how modern-day slavery is distinct from traditional antebellum slavery.

Slavery in Florida

The history of slavery in Florida is not completely distinct from the various forms of slavery that were historically established throughout what would become the United States. For the first two centuries of Spanish control of Florida, indigenous young men were forced to plant and harvest corn so that the colonizers could be fed. By 1763, when Great Britain gained control of the Florida territory, enslaved Africans were the primary source of labor. Prior to the Civil War, two forms of forced labor were established. The first of these was the traditional antebellum slavery evident in other parts of the country. The other form of labor was known as "pushing." According to a booklet of the Florida Modern-Day Slavery Museum (2010), pushing was established when "transitory planters sought to maximize their wealth by extracting greater speeds of labor from their enslaved workers and constantly increasing maximum production requirements" (2). Documents from this period described pushing as a new form of slavery as well as a new form of torture.

After the 1865 passage of the Thirteenth Amendment, which permanently ended the institution of chattel slavery throughout the country, slavery in Florida was transformed. The two main forms that were established were the convict release system and peonage. The convict release system was an agreement between prisons and the state whereby convicts were released to work on farms or in the mines. The prisoners were expendable in that they could easily be replaced. As one farmer remarked about the new form of labor during this time:

> Before the war, we owned the negroes. If a man had a good nigger, he could afford to take care of him...But these convicts: we don't own

'em. One dies, get another. (Quoted in Florida Modern-Day Slavery Museum 2010: 3)

The other form of slavery that became widely used was peonage. The most common form of peonage was associated with sharecroppers and "the state's most undesirable and lowest-paid workplaces" (ibid.: 4). Specifically, the turpentine industry was widely known for hiring vulnerably low-paid workers. Workers were required to slash pine trees and extract the gum, and then transport the material to the factories where the gum was separated into tar and rosin. The work conditions were harsh as workers toiled in the heat, bodies caked in sticky gum and hot tar.

By the twentieth century, technology expanded the production and distribution of citrus fruit, sugarcane, and vegetables in central and south Florida, which created a need for cheap labor that would be available only during the harvest season, migrating to other jobs at the end of the season. Thus, "Florida's agricultural firms recruited harvesters from the chaos of Georgia's imploding sharecropping system. These workers…pieced together an annual migration circuit by harvesting crops along the Eastern seaboard" (ibid.: 5). Florida farms had officially become dependent on migrant labor.

From the 1940s through the 1980s, debt peonage reemerged among the migrant laborers, but it had evolved into a new form. Migrants would incur debt through forced living conditions. Workers would rent their living quarters from the employer, as well as buy their food and other commodities from the company store. Prices were extremely inflated, and therefore, the minimal pay the workers received did not measure up to the debt that was owed for rent and items bought in the company store. In order to repay the debt, the workers had to worker harder and longer hours as the debt trap constructed by the employer became more difficult to escape. It is this form of peonage that has continued to persist into the twenty-first century in the migrant camps of southern Florida.

Today, there exist three main differences between modern-day slavery and traditional slavery. The first of these is that the enslaved people of today are hidden from the public eye and are closely monitored by the slavers. Long gone are the days when slave labor was part of the roadside landscape, for today the agricultural field laborers invisibly toil in hidden fields well beyond the beaten path. One is not going to drive through the town of Immokalee and see the victims of forced labor in their labor environment. In fact, aside from the pinhooking market, there is no real indication that the majority of tomatoes in the United States are harvested just beyond the outskirts of this unassuming town. The tomato fields are miles outside of Immokalee, off back roads that are relatively untraveled with the exception of the labor buses. The farmworkers are not seen and the rationale behind hiding the enslaved workers is to reinforce the assumption that slavery no longer exists in the United States. As long as passers-by cannot see the reality, the reality does not exist.

The second difference between modern-day slavery and the traditional forms of slavery is that today, coercion, force, and threat of force are virtually the only means of controlling the slaves. Although there are accounts of individuals being physically restrained by chains or held at gunpoint by armed guards, more often enslaved victims are subjected to constant threats of force to their own personhood, as well as to their families still living in their country of origin. These threats, in addition to an insurmountable debt, are what maintain the system of captivity. There is also an element physical force when laborers "violate" the rules, as when trying to escape. Unlike in the traditional model of slavery, modern-day slavery is maintained through a psychological warfare developed through deception, surveillance, and intimidation, rather than with chains and cages.

The third difference is that in modern forms of slavery, the enslaved victims are expected to repay the costs associated with the nature of their slavery. Whereas historically slaves were bought and had not incurred any debt, today, victims of slavery are expected to pay for their travel to the United States, their housing, their food, their equipment for work, and any other costs that may have accrued during transportation and employment. In most cases, identification papers are confiscated until the debt is repaid but repayment is virtually impossible, for as soon as the debt is close to being paid back to the trafficker, another "cost" suddenly accrues. Although uniquely different, modern-day slavery needs to be recognized for what it is. Individuals are being coerced to labor under the harshest of work conditions for little to no pay. They are physically and psychologically abused, and they are unable to escape until they have met the demands of the traffickers. Socially, many want to call it by another, less loaded name, but despite the differences, human trafficking is slavery.

Slavery in Immokalee

Visiting the town of Immokalee, it is difficult to fathom that for eight months of the year, this is predominantly an agricultural migrant community. The town is small, and there are virtually no fields to harvest. There are factories at the edge of town that finalize the production of produce, and there is a pinhooking market selling the leftovers of the daily harvest, but there are no visible fields within the city limits. This is because the fields are located miles outside of town on back roads that are difficult to navigate for drivers who do not regularly travel them. If one were able to stumble upon a tomato field, there would seem to be nothing more than a botanical wall or fence, which obstructs any view of the workers. Entry is available to a select few, as hired security block the entrance.

Even if a glimpse may be caught of the workers, the first view of slavery is so overwhelming that the workers become one a single mass of generalizable characteristics. From this distant perspective, the workers, wearing baseball caps to offer some protection from the sun, appear to be the same height. Skin is blistered and browned; hands are calloused and permanently blackened by the soil. Heads hang low as tomatoes are picked and buckets are hoisted and carried on shoulders. The workers become one, but each individual is unique in his own experience. However, as an outsider, I am unable to move beyond this quick glimpse of the enslaved farmworkers, for the farmers and the field bosses assure that this forced labor will remain hidden one way or another.

Because of the obstacles of entry and observation of the migrant workers in the field, I employed alternative methods to develop a clear image of who is working in the fields. I observed the early evening drop-off of workers by the labor buses, and I analyzed the demographic information revealed in arrest reports, including occupation, age, and country of origin. With this methodology, I was able to develop a typology of the field workers based on age, gender, and country of origin.

Upon analysis, it is apparent that the majority of the workers in the fields share a number of common characteristics that would make it convenient to lump them into a homogenous group, which can be both beneficial and detrimental. On the one hand, to categorize the workers as a single unit makes it more favorable to generalize their experiences to the whole. Conversely, to generalize the experiences of the workers as a single faction limits their individuality and reduces them to a group more easily ignored. Therefore, I have focused on the commonalities that establish the shared experiences of the workers, but at the same time, I have created a distinct typology that differentiates the workers in terms of their work responsibilities, criminality, and individual protection. Although this typology is not entire in its explanation to the extent of diversities evident within the community of farmworkers, it offers an insight into the individual differences and consequent experiences that are often overlooked when discussing modern-day slavery.

The most apparent similarity among the workers is the country of origin. An overwhelming majority of the field workers are from either Mexico or Guatemala. This is not surprising, for national research has identified Mexico and Guatemala as top origin countries for victims trafficked into the United States (see Free the Slaves). Focusing just on the migrant population of Immokalee, arrest reports reveal that approximately 70 percent of the identified farmworkers are Mexican, while another 12 percent of the identified field laborers are from Guatemala.[1] However, a small percentage of the workers within the tomato industry are from Haiti and other neighboring countries.

The Haitian workers have a unique experience compared to the Mexican, Guatemalan, and other Central and South American workers in that most of the Haitian workers are found within the production factories rather than the fields. When inquiring about why the Haitians would more likely be found in the factories, I received two different types of responses. Some believe that the reason Haitians are working in the factories is solely their race. More than once, I was told that those who designate work responsibilities believe that migrant workers of Hispanic origin are more likely to tolerate the heat and be more laborious in the fields than the Haitians. In other words, "the Haitians are lazy." On the other hand, because the Hispanic workers are "less likely to complain" about the grueling work conditions, they are placed in the fields, whereas the protesting Haitians are placed in the factories. Of course, this is racist speculation with no basis in reality, but it is an unfortunate stereotype held by a handful of the farm handlers.

The other response regarding labor designation, one I believe to be more relevant to reality, recognizes the method of transportation into the United States as a crucial labor indicator. Although there is an obvious racial discrepancy in terms of labor responsibilities, not all migrating Haitians who arrive in Immokalee find themselves in the production factories. Some do work in the fields, and this is mainly due to whether the movement across the border was the result of trafficking or smuggling. To reiterate, the key difference between smuggling and trafficking is volition on the part of the individual being moved. Those who are smuggled have voluntarily paid a transporter to assist in border crossing, and are left to their own devices when they safely step on U.S. soil. Those who are trafficked are coerced into coming to the United States and are trapped in a system of bondage until the debt to the trafficker is repaid. Because of the difference in transportation method, those who have been smuggled have more freedom in choosing their occupation.

A history of state violence, military coups, and economic instability has triggered a virtually constant exodus of Haitian people to the United States. One of the larger arrivals occurred in the early 1990s when tens of thousands of exiled Aristide supporters landed on U.S. shores (Kyle and Scarcelli 2009). More recently, the United States has seen a surge of Haitian migrants escaping the earthquake-devastated country in search of a new and improved life. In most of these cases, the Haitian migrant has voluntarily paid a smuggler to assist in the treacherous boat journey, and is left to find work independently upon arrival. Because of this independence, many of the Haitians who find their way to southern Florida are able to find work in the factories rather than the fields. Those who are trafficked into southern Florida, on the other hand, are without options and are more likely to be forced to work in the fields by the traffickers and field bosses.

Whether because of racist stereotypes or the method of transportation into the United States, it is apparent that the Haitian workers involved in the tomato industry experience work conditions much different from their Hispanic counterparts. The work in the factories is less brutal than the field labor due to the fact that the factories are more visible and surveilled by company officials. Once the tomatoes reach the stage of packing and distribution, there is a level of labor compliance that must be established, for the farmers have a more direct link to this line of production. In the fields, the farmers allow for field bosses to regulate labor and responsibilities, and thus they can rely on ignorance and deniability when approached with accusations of slave labor. This is not to say that the Haitians working in the production factories have high-end work conditions, for the hours are long, the factories are hot, and the pay is minimal. Yet, the workers in the factories experience a sense of security and freedom in comparison to those working to pay off a trafficking debt.

Regardless of country of origin, the vast majority of workers are men. In fact, only two women were identified as field laborers in my analysis. Of course, it can be easily concluded that more than two women are working in the fields, but women are more likely to have other occupations if trafficked into Immokalee. For the most part, the women trafficked into Immokalee (and the United States in general) are victims of the forced commercial sex industry (See Chapter 3). Many times, overlapping with the forced commercial sex industry, women will also be forced to work as domestic servants. In other cases, women remain in the country of origin while their husbands and/or sons are working in the United States. These women are waiting for their partners to become established in their careers before they travel across the borders. Once they are in the States, the traditional patriarchy limits the work of many women to stay-at-home mothers. Women in this situation are more likely to be smuggled rather than trafficked into the United States, with their situation being forced by their male family members rather than the traffickers. Chapter 3 will provide a more detailed analysis of the trafficked women in Immokalee, but for the purposes of the typology of field workers, it is imperative to recognize the apparent gender profile of the farmworkers.

Finally, among the male Mexican and Guatemalan workers there is a major age differential, with some workers being in their sixties while others are in their teens; the average age is approximately thirty-one. Age, in general, is an interesting phenomenon that is associated with legislation regarding trafficking. A young child who is identified selling sexual services, regardless of immigration status or the voluntariness of the services, is automatically considered a victim of trafficking due to the age of consent. On the other hand, children identified as farmworkers are not automatically identified as victims of human trafficking. In fact, they are first identified as criminals due to their undocumented status, and it is the child's responsibility to prove that he is a victim of trafficking rather than being an undocumented worker voluntarily choosing to assist in agricultural labor.

In the agricultural slavery evident in Immokalee, age is the most compelling distinction in terms of the workers' experience. This is because the worker's age is a determinant of the level of familiarity with migrant work and the scope of migrant protection received from external groups. The age of the farmworker also reveals a pattern of ignorance regarding issues of visibility and the repercussions to being identified as an undocumented worker.

Arrest records reveal that younger migrants are more likely than their older counterparts to be identified for criminal behavior. Older workers who are identified are usually arrested when among a group of other workers, and are most likely guilty of "open container" violations. Young workers, on the other hand, are more likely to be arrested for driving violations and physical altercations. This is an important distinction, because it is illustrative that the older workers who have experience in the cycle of migration have learned that in order to continue working, they must not engage in criminal behavior. Due to stringent immigration laws (See Chapter 4), it is important for the farmworkers to be identified as community members rather than part of a criminal element.

In line with the legal naivety of young workers is the relationship of trust established between the migrant workers and the police. Initially, the young workers have very little trust for the local law enforcement. They have been told repeatedly by their traffickers (and more recently by some advocates) that the police conduct secret raids with the aim of arresting and deporting undocumented workers. This in turn creates a divide between the workers and the local police, so that the police are unable to identify and protect the victims of trafficking. Those who have returned to Immokalee each harvest season have somewhat come to terms with the notion that the police are willing to assist victims, but this minimal foundation of trust must be established each year with new and young workers. From this evolves the problematic contradiction that the police are attempting to create a community of trust and protection among the workers, but the young workers continue to find themselves arrested and eligible for deportation, thereby fracturing attempts of confidence in police protection.

A final distinction with respect to age and experience is that returning workers have established networks of external protection beyond the scope of the local police. This protection is developed from grassroots organizations advocating workers' rights. The most prominent of these is the Coalition of Immokalee Workers (CIW) (See Chapter 5). Workers who receive the assistance of advocacy groups such as the CIW reap small benefits that allow for improved working conditions and minimal pay increases. Young workers with no ties to the established migrant community are unlikely to be aware of this external support and the benefits of connecting oneself to an advocacy-based organization. The end result is a divide of worker experiences in the field. Those who utilize external movements establish a sense of visibility and the consequential response of somewhat improved work conditions and pay. Those workers independent of any sort of external support find themselves in a socially unsupervised environment much more conducive to abuse. Many times, it is only when their plight becomes horrific that they become socially visible and in turn recognize the importance of relying on networks of protection and support. It is this divide that is central to the typology of workers.

Based on the demographic characteristics of workers, I have separated the workers into two categories according to a hierarchical arrangement of power. Following a Domhoffian (1990) ideal model, I distinguish two types of power developed though external protection: economic and political.[2] Economic power is simply connected to wages earned for field labor. For example, those workers that exhibit economic power are able to benefit financially, even if it is simply a penny more per pound of tomatoes picked. Political power is defined as the ability to alter, create, or terminate policy with regards to labor conditions. In other words, political power is the ability to train the national spotlight on the plight of the farmworkers, forcing the hand of the farmer to provide better work conditions for his employees. Each of these systems is dependent on external support and protection. Utilizing these systems of power, the analysis revealed that those workers with ties to external support networks are more able to improve their work and life conditions than those who are independent of any assistance.

Each system of power is fused with the other in complex ways, thereby influencing where the farmworkers are placed on a stratified power hierarchy. Those with no external system of support are considered to be part of the lower order of the stratified system and exhibit little or no source of power. In other words, these workers do not have the ability to change labor policy or demand a pay increase. They are virtually invisible until their experience becomes so horrific that the external agencies identify them as victims of modern-day slavery, and they are then able to climb the hierarchy to join those workers who enjoy external support and assistance. Unfortunately, it is not until the point of almost total devastation that those workers with no external ties enjoy the benefits of support.

Recall the incident described in the introduction of this volume, with the workers who were chained to the inside a boxcar for years. The case of these workers is a clear example of the torturous conditions that arise if a worker is unable to rely on protection through advocates and legal groups. The life and work conditions are deplorable, and the only chance of improvement is through a relatively impossible escape. The workers with no external assistance are invisible, and if something were to happen to them, no one would know.

Those with ties to external networks are considered to be at the top of the system not only through possessing some level of power, but also by utilizing this power to their own benefit. Some of these benefits include media coverage and public recognition of the farmworkers' plight, as well as mediations with farm owners. These workers are visible, and gain the recognition of national and international media outlets. With such pressure from networks outside the borders of Immokalee, farmers are pressured to improve the work and life conditions of the employees. However, the pressure may be alleviated if the farmer is able to rely on deniability of slavery, while at the same time increasing security to keep prying eyes away from the fields. Therefore, this system results in a fragmentation of experiences whereby some farmworkers have small demands met, while other workers must endure the most horrific of work conditions.

One may question why a farmworker would not immediately seek out assistance upon arrival in Immokalee. The answer to this is threefold. The first reason many workers do not seek out network support is their lack of knowledge that such a network exists. This is especially true now that immigration enforcement in Immokalee is becoming stricter. Many of the workers now live in nearby towns with less scrutiny by federal immigration authorities and are bused to the Immokalee fields. Therefore, the migrant workers do not spend as much time in Immokalee to learn about organizations such as the CIW, and consequently do not realize that there is an outlet for support.

The second reason that many workers do not seek out external support is because they are fearful of strangers, especially strangers who are legal citizens. Despite their efforts to improve the life of the agricultural laborers, gaining the workers' trust is difficult because many of the volunteers with the CIW and other advocacy based organizations are legal citizens. Some of these volunteers were once farmworkers themselves that have successfully gained citizenship in the United States, while others are natural citizens who are sympathetic to the plight of the workers. In any case, the advocates are legal citizens and are therefore felt to be a threat by the farmworkers. The migrant laborers have been conditioned by their traffickers to not trust anyone, for even the friendliest face may be a ruse to initiate the deportation of undocumented workers.

Finally, some workers may decline the assistance of an external organization for the mere reason that it is too much of a hassle. As noted by Bowe (2007),

> workers have little energy for conversation with strangers after a day of intense manual labor. For another [thing], most immigrant workers are loath to fraternize with anyone who might bring headaches into their lives. They simply want to work, pay off the money they've borrowed to come here, and start sending money back home to their families (26).

Regardless of the reason, the end result of not relying on external assistance is a reality of mental and physical abuse.

Although I have emphasized the individual experiences of the migrant workers, there is a generalizable working environment. It has been noted that some workers may benefit from external support, thereby receiving a little more pay with less abusive conditions, but overall, the plight of the workers remains deplorable as they labor in intense heat, with little to no water, under extreme hours and conditions.

The Work Experience of the Agricultural Slave

According to the CIW, "Southwest Florida is the state's most important center for agricultural production, and Immokalee is the state's largest farm worker community" (ciw-online.org, accessed April, 2009). In fact, "as much as 90 percent of the fresh domestic tomatoes we eat come from south Florida" (Estabrook 2009; Estabrook 2011). Because of this agricultural hub, southern Florida is a hot-spot destination for thousands of undocumented migrant farmworkers. In fact, "80 percent of the migrants in Florida are illegal immigrants and thus especially vulnerable to abuse" (Schlosser 2007), including low wages, intolerable conditions, and virtually no legal protection. According to Bowe:

> The average migrant has a life expectancy of just forty-nine years. Twenty thousand farm workers require medical treatment for acute pesticide poisoning each year; at least that many more cases go unreported...An estimated 80 percent [of Florida farm workers] have no work papers, and...their average yearly pay [is] an estimated $6,574 (2007: 8)

The work is literally backbreaking, as laborers must carry and unload approximately two tons of tomatoes a day just to elevate their earnings to a minimum wage payday.[3] In general, the workday begins at five in the morning; potential workers wait over an hour for a contractor to choose who will work in the fields that day. The farmworkers cannot pick any tomatoes until the morning dew has been burned off by the sun, so they must wait until approximately 9:00 am before they can begin the picking process. This waiting period is unpaid. Once they are able to begin picking the tomatoes, the workers must engage in the constant choreography of bending down to pick the tomato and then placing the tomato in a basket. Once the basket is full, the workers hoist it onto their shoulders and must run the tomatoes to the truck without spilling or damaging the product. This dance is performed for hours on end with no time for a break.

The afternoon routine differs depending on the level of external protection the worker enjoys. Workers with influential citizens lobbying on their behalf do earn a midday break for lunch. This lunch is eaten as quickly as possible, for the farmworkers are losing money by not continuing the tomato-picking cycle. Along with the time constraint, there are usually no facilities on the farms, and so workers do not get a chance to wash their hand before eating. Therefore, workers must consume their lunch with hands covered in pesticides.

The workers who do not benefit from external support networks may not receive a midday break. These workers may dare to eat a small snack in between tomato runs. However, this attempt could lead to negative results such as physical abuse by a field boss, or complete termination from work and loss of pay. Of course, a worker who chooses not to eat and continues to work risks heat exhaustion. In even more extreme situations, the worker will not have access to clean water on the farm. These workers have actually succumbed to drinking water from an irrigation ditch just to find some relief from the extreme heat.

After the midday break, the farmworkers must return to the picking ritual. As the sun smolders throughout the afternoon, the workers must continue to pick tomatoes and run to the trucks until approximately 5:00 pm. If the season produces an especially abundant harvest, workers may continue to pick the tomatoes until it becomes dark and visibility is completely lost. Due to the hidden nature of agricultural slavery, the field bosses will not invest in lighting, for this could draw attention to nighttime labor. Therefore, the workday is dependent on sunlight, and as long as there is still some light and tomatoes to be harvested, the work will continue well into the darkness.

At the end of the workday, the exhausted workers climb aboard the labor buses and are returned to their point of original departure; each worker is then responsible for finding a way home for the night. The farm-owned housing is coincidentally placed within walking distance of the drop-off point. Because of lack of transportation beyond walking, many workers are forced to reside in the homes regulated by farmers. The housing system is an ingenious effort on the part of the farmers in that they are able to perpetuate free labor because they control the cost of rent. Regardless of how many hours have been worked, the debt cycle is constant, for, on average, a worker who picks 4,000 pounds of tomatoes earns a mere $50 for the day. The reality is that to pick two tons of tomatoes is relatively impossible. The majority of the workers are weakened due to lack of food and water in addition to heat exhaustion. Even if a worker is able to garner enough strength to harvest without hesitation, there may not be two tons of tomatoes available for picking. Regardless, if a worker is able to collect the $50 pay at the end of a workday, that salary is recycled back to the farmer in the form of rent while the debt to the trafficker remains unpaid. This in turn perpetuates a system of forced free labor.

Social Restraints

Defining this work as modern-day slavery conjures up images of chains and physical imprisonment. Although rare, as already indicated, this has been the case for some victims of trafficking. Local law enforcement and advocates have discovered workers chained inside a 24-foot box truck, forced to sleep, eat, shower, and defecate in "private" corners, as illustrated by the case study in the introduction. In other cases, "workers were held against their will through threats, drugs, beatings, shootings, and pistol-whippings" (Heuvel 2010: 1). Others are kept under constant watch by armed guards, making escape virtually impossible. Some of the identified workers had been held in these atrocious conditions for eleven years before they either escaped or were discovered. Today, there exists a modern slavery museum reproducing the conditions, and visitors have described the experience as "unbearable." As one visitor described a visit to a reproduction of the living quarters of a group of identified victims, "'The stale air was uncomfortable to breathe. Sweat soaked to the back of my shirt. And I was in there for less than five minutes, not two and a half years'" (quoted in Heuvel 2010).

The above examples are cases that will generate media attention when identified; however, in general, the majority of the workers in Immokalee are not physically imprisoned, but are rather confined by three social restraints that are inherent in human trafficking. The first of these is an economic restraint. Due to the virtual impossibility of picking two tons of tomatoes five days a week, the workers' salary averages approximately $548 a month, which must be used to pay for rent, food, utilities, as well as a payment to a trafficker or *coyote* who has assisted in the border crossing. Workers may arrive in the States already thousands of dollars in debt. Once here, the debt increases dramatically with inflated rent and high prices of food.

According to Detective Charlie Frost's statement before the Senate Committee on Health, Education, Labor, and Pensions:

> [T]raffickers…hold a victim in a system perpetually accruing debt. Victims have incurred debts for housing, food, water, and transportation. In one instance, victims related to me that they were charged for three days worth of wages if they were sick for one day and could not work. This of course is added to the debt then subtracted from what the victims have earned at the end of the week. Victims earning a dollar per bucket of picked tomatoes can work for the full week and receive nothing more than twenty dollars from the trafficker at the end of the week (Frost 2008).

Many of the workers are forced to live in what can only be described as modern company towns. The housing conditions rival that of a third world country. Overgrown landscape, broken shutters, and peeling paint are common to many of the homes. Some of these homes are actually backyard sheds that had been modified into living units. Most are one- or two-room units with four to eight people living together, although some homes have offered residency to up to twelve workers living in a one-bedroom unit. Curtains become walls to afford some sense of privacy. A large percentage of the housing is owned and rent is regulated by the farmers. Because options are limited, the rent escalates to a fee that is virtually impossible to pay on the minimal salary workers receive. Rent may range anywhere from $40 to $150 a week, depending on the type of housing, as well as the number of inhabitants.

In addition to the rent, the local merchants are aware that there is limited competition for commodities, so prices are inflated. Grocery shopping does not proceed by the American middle-class system of buying food and household items for a number of upcoming days; rather, food is bought a meal at a time. This is to ensure that the meal can be afforded. A pseudo-credit system exists for some of the returning workers who reside in Immokalee and are known to the merchants. Of course there is no legality to this system, and it is all "under the table," leaving the system open to abuse by the merchants, for credit from the merchant is most certain to come with a high-interest repayment. If the workers have access to transportation, they are able to escape the independent merchants and shop from the chain stores on the other side of town. Of course, this causes the workers to be dependent on the chain store prices, as well as the inability to borrow what is needed for the day.

The CIW has approached the problem associated with high-cost commodities by offering a variety of staple items at a lower cost at the central headquarters. Unfortunately, as with all other issues associated with external support, the benefit of lower cost items is only available to those who have the knowledge that such items exist. Therefore, if workers are unaware of the option of shopping at the CIW headquarters, they are unable to benefit from this assistance.

The two other social restraints that maintain the system of slavery are physical and psychological. According to one detective I spoke with, the workers are almost completely imprisoned by psychological chains. "Traffickers create an environment of fear meant to control their victims." There are no gates to keep the workers from escaping, but the workers are aware of the penalty if they escape and are caught. The detective continued:

> If a worker escapes and is found, he will be brought back [to the farm] by the slavers. At the farm, the other workers must stop what they are doing and watch as the man who tried to escape is beaten by three or four [handlers]. You have to remember that the worker is small and weak. The men beating him are sometimes three times his size.

The beatings are meant to be imprinted into the minds of the other workers and are a lesson to anyone else who tries to escape. For some, the stories passed down regarding the punishment for escape are enough to keep the workers from leaving before paying off their debt. Just the knowledge that this is a potential result, whether real or a story told through the seasons, creates enough psychological stress to rule out a chance of escape.

Other than the beatings (or threat of a beating), the workers face immense fear for their families in their country of origin. Both victim advocates and legal professionals report that the workers will not speak out against their handlers because of the direct ties to their families. Traffickers have either directly stated or insinuated to the farmworkers that if they try to turn to the local police for assistance, their families will be murdered. This is usually not an empty threat because of the relationship between many of the workers and the traffickers. Successful traffickers build a network of "friendship" before assistance in border crossing is offered. In a number of cases, the identified trafficker was actually found to be an extended family member or longtime family friend to the trafficked victim. Although less likely in agricultural slavery, some of the younger workers have been sold to the traffickers by their parents. In most trafficking cases, the traffickers have developed a relationship with the family members remaining in the country of origin. This relationship ensures an element of control over the workers, as they realize that their families are under surveillance and are in danger if the worker crosses the trafficker.

Workers also face the fear of deportation. Although the officers attempt to communicate that the workers will not be deported if they cooperate with the police in detaining a trafficker, the language barrier causes an immense problem. For example, an officer may not speak Spanish (the native language of a large percentage of the workers). Many times, if the officer does speak Spanish, it still does not benefit the communication, for many of the workers speak a dialect specific to indigenous groups of Mexico or Guatemala. Officers attempt to work with translators, but this is not always plausible. Therefore, the officers must depend on a willing bilingual individual to assist in the interview. As one officer explained, "usually when English speaking officers go out to a scene, they're very happy to have somebody who offers to translate for them. In a slavery situation, the person that's going to offer to translate for them is [most likely] part of the slavery organization." In other words, the willing individual is most likely part of the trafficking ring. Because of the language barrier, the translator is able to imitate police assistance while he/she is speaking to the migrant worker explaining that the police are there to advocate for deportation, thereby obstructing any possible cooperation on the part of the victim. Police are aware of this dilemma, and have made attempts to use the services of the human trafficking advocate (who is bilingual), but resources are limited, and there remains the issue of not knowing the indigenous dialect.

Workers also suffer abuse from one another and local citizens from Immokalee and neighboring communities. One of the most common types of victimization is referred to as the "guato-lotto," or the Guatemalan lottery. According to an officer:

> The [workers]…have no place to put their money. They don't want to leave their money at home in their mattress because of their roommate…You know they live with 6, 8 other men, they fear the roommate will steal the money while they are gone. So, they carry [the cash] around in their pockets. Well, they go out, and they get stupid drunk, walk home, and you just shove them down and take their money. It's the guato-lotto—you get the lottery.

Most of this type of activity is "migrant on migrant" crime, and generally theft is "for some of the silliest stuff" such as beer money. Unfortunately, there is no real solution to migrant theft. Because they are undocumented, the workers do not have the luxury of putting their earnings in a bank. Therefore, the workers face a constant risk of having their salaries stolen at the end of the workday. It is a risk that has become inherent to the lives of migrant farmworkers in Immokalee.

An interesting phenomenon has occurred in terms of who is restraining the workers in the field, for there exists a labor hierarchy among the undocumented workers. This hierarchy is based on certain workers building a system of trust and support from both the senior field bosses and the farmers themselves. Trust and support for laborers are developed through a number of means, including returning to work for the same farmer year after year, paying off the trafficking debt, and acquiring citizenship. Whatever the reason, some workers are able to climb the "labor ladder" and move beyond working as a field laborer toward becoming a field boss.

Promotion of farmworkers to the level of field boss is important to the maintenance of slavery in the fields for three reasons. The first is trust. Many of the workers are acquainted with the field bosses before they cross the border, for as earlier stated, the field boss may be a family friend or relative. This eases but does not eliminate the coercion element of trafficking, for the farmworkers believe that they will find work in the States that will enable them to bring their family across the border. Of course, once they cross the border, they are blindsided with debt bondage and horrific work conditions from which they are unable to escape. Other workers see the field boss as an ally, for the boss comes from the same migrant farming class as the worker. Building on this trust, field bosses are able to employ mechanisms of control, which is the second element in maintenance of slavery.

Control is directly linked to the three restraints previously discussed. Because the workers trust the field bosses as friends and/or family, the "truths" regarding local threats becomes so ingrained in many of the workers' minds that they refuse to turn to external support to escape the system of slavery. Many of the workers come to the States, and the only relationships they have are with the traffickers. They have been repeatedly told from before the border crossing and upon arrival to trust no one else, for the threat of deportation is real. Once here, they are left with no resources and a great debt to repay. The workers immediately jump into the day-to-day activities and focus only on work, hoping not to be noticed; being noticed could lead to termination or deportation. The psychological and economical restraints are maintained by the trust in a "friendship" of those who hold the power to restrain.

The field boss's control is fundamental not only to the workers who have just crossed the border, but also to those workers that migrate to Immokalee each harvest season. Of course, some who return may climb the hierarchy and become a field boss themselves, but others become accommodated to the way power is structured in Immokalee. Being aware of the various facets of power, the older, returning migrants can easily succumb to the psychological restraints. For returning workers who have not yet paid off their debt nor achieved citizenship, there always exists the constant threat of deportation, termination, and abuse, so that many of the returning workers view the field bosses as an undeniable threat that must be accepted. Resistance is most certain to end in some form of discomfort for the worker.

Finally, the field bosses serve to maintain and secure the system of slavery while the farmers enjoy invisible deniability of the atrocities occurring on their fields. Farmers hire the field bosses to hire the field laborers. This is ingenious on the part of the farmers; when they are confronted with accusations of slave labor, they simply state that they do not hire the field laborers. This work is entrusted to the documented field bosses, and who the field bosses hire is completely beyond the control of the farmer. Therefore, when the accusations become criminal charges, the deniability leads to an arrest and prosecution of the field boss(es) rather than the farmer who hires the field bosses. This has led to a number of successful prosecutions of abusive field bosses, but at the time of this writing, no farmer has yet been prosecuted for the slavery that is evident in the Immokalee fields.

The Persistence of Slavery

Legally, small steps are being taken to reduce the instances of extreme abuse in Immokalee, but the question still remains as to why, in the twenty-first century, agricultural slavery persists. The answer is the same as it historically has always been. Slavery is acceptable as long as the larger society benefits from the exploitation, and those who are exploited are presumed to be a disposable population. In order to fully understand why slavery continues to exist in the United States, a brief discussion of the evolution of slavery in the modern sense is helpful.

Most readers are familiar with the various forms of slavery that have existed throughout history and have evolved in the modern world. Traditionally, slavery in the United States has been understood as the slavery of Africans prior to the Civil War. Images of chained bondage and physical beatings while men and women toiled in the fields have been illustrated both through visual media and academic history. However, slavery, although constitutionally abolished, continued to exist in various forms following the passage of the Thirteenth Amendment.

After the Civil War slave-like labor took on a variety of forms, including indentured labor, free labor, and contract labor. In the United States, the majority of those affected by these new labor practices were former Black slaves and German, Irish, and Chinese immigrants. In the former Confederate South, Black Codes were adopted, which were applied "specifically to African Americans, whose central feature was the imposition of criminal prosecution for those who failed to sign one-year labor contracts, or who had left a job after they had signed such a contract" (Montgomery 1993: 37). The criminal penalties resulted in the overflow of jails, thereby allowing for the "criminal" to serve his punishment in the form of free labor either in the agricultural or domestic arenas. Congress took a strong stance against the Southern Black Codes, and the Codes were legally abolished in 1866.

Following the various Southern slave agendas, a movement toward contract labor was developed.

> Contract labour can be described as one mode along a spectrum of forms of migration, permanent and temporary, whose purpose is to move populations from one area to another, and, possibly, to influence (or limit) the selection of occupations after arrival. It combines characteristics of free and involuntary migration... (Engerman 1986: 267).

Contract labor is most similar to modern forms of slavery and human trafficking, yet the element of coercion has historically "been a subject of controversy" (ibid.: 267). Such labor was considered to be free in the sense that the laborer had the illusion that he could "commodify or recommodify labor power at any moment in the agricultural cycle" (Brass 1999: 10), but if the worker is restrained by any debt owed to the employer, the worker is not considered to be truly free. It was this system of "debt repayment" that set the foundation for the sense of bonded labor that is central to modern-day slavery.

Debt bondage is defined as

> circumstances where cash loans advanced by a creditor...are repaid in the form of labour-service, by the debtor personally and/or by members of his domestic/affinal/fictive kin group...Where the creditor does not personally own land...the labour-power of a debtor may be profitably leased to a third party that does. In contexts where the lender is only or also a proprietor who hires in workers..., the labour-power of debtors will be employed on those holding under his control... (ibid.: 11)

Debt bondage in its early forms was extended both to immigrant and American-born laborers. Specifically, hoboes (i.e., drifters) and the other members of the migrant class from the 1880s to the 1930s, all of whom were regarded an indispensible labor class, were caught in the cycle of debt bondage.

As this brief history highlights, slavery, in all forms (including migrant labor and indentured servitude), has been the backbone of American capitalism and consumerism. The product resulting from slave labor has continued to be affordable for the American public, and as long as the goods are consumed, the slavery persists. This is especially true in a time of economic crisis when families are dependent on cheap commodities to meet their needs.

Traditionally, the system of cheap goods has taken a variety of forms, including but not limited to sugar, cotton, greenery, gems, fruit, and vegetables. In Immokalee, the tomato industry flourishes as the fruits are shipped and found on dinner tables throughout the United States. To reiterate, almost 90 percent of the domestic tomatoes we eat come from Florida, and "Immokalee is the tomato capital of the United States" (Estabrook 2009: 1). Therefore, a large percentage of Americans are eating tomatoes that have been harvested in Immokalee by the undocumented workers struggling to survive in slave-like conditions. Although the plight of the worker has been publicly discussed in documentaries, magazines, books, and other media outlets, many turn a blind eye to the slavery in our own back yard. Reasons for denial may include guilt, convenience, and cost. Many individuals may not want to think about the process that goes into getting food to their table every day. Others find it convenient to buy Florida tomatoes from the local grocer in the middle of winter rather than hunting down tomatoes identified as "slave-free." Finally, utilizing slave labor keeps the cost of tomatoes down all year round. Most Americans, especially in a modern economic crisis, do not want to pay a high price per pound of tomatoes, which would be the reality if the workers were paid a legal wage for their labor.

Aside from the consumerism of the tomatoes, the other factor that allows for the persistence of slavery in the Immokalee fields is the identity of those actually being exploited. In a time of anti-immigrant sentiment and border control, it is difficult for many Americans to feel sympathy for an "illegal" population. In fact, many argue that the agricultural workers came here "voluntarily," and if they are unhappy with their situation, they should "go home." For example, following a news article on modern slavery in Immokalee (Williams 2010), some of the following comments were made:

> "They are taking a chance coming into this or any country illegally."
> "Deport all illegals [sic] and the problem is solved."
> "If they enter here illegally then they should be exploited."

This is a common theme among people posting comments publicly; however, there is also support for the workers, represented by such comments as: "Whoa, another really good reason to grow your own tomatoes" and "That is so fucked!" Unfortunately, the anti-immigrant sentiment that screams so loudly on blogs, in comment sections, and through day-to-day interaction provides rationalization for the slavery. In other words, as with many forms of vulnerable populations being victimized, it is much easier to blame the victim rather than look at the institutional structure that supports and accepts slavery. In the United States, that institutional structure is a combination of convenient consumerism, a southern border secured from an undesirable element, and capitalist profit.

Conclusion

Toward the end of the nineteenth century and into the twentieth century, "millions of people worked in highly seasonal occupations, piecing together a living by whatever means they could" (Higbie 2003: 2). During this period, the migrant class was composed of immigrant and American born "homeless drifters." These workers were feared by their drifter persona, yet needed for their cheap labor, and therefore became regarded as the "'indispensible outcasts of rural America'" (quoted in Higbie 2003: 3). The migrating hoboes (drifters) were exploited and abused by their employers to the point that the migrants realized the only way to escape the oppressive conditions was to merge as a united class. Eventually, the hoboes represented a revolutionary force, announcing the ultimatum that they would transfer their labor to urban industrialization if they did not receive better wages. This in turn would adversely affect the rural sector by eliminating the requisite hands-on labor.

At the same time farmers were utilizing the cheap U.S. migrant labor, Mexican migrants were also being exploited in the agricultural sector. As explained by Tuirán:

> The first wave of migrant workers to the U.S. were comprised of: experienced miners, work hands from the cattle ranches in the states of Sonora, Chihuahua, Coahuila, and Tamaulipas, indentured servants which were fleeing Mexican traditional farms, small independent producers who were affected by natural disasters or by Indian raids, and workers who were attracted by the War of Secession, the flowering sale of Mexican border locales and which because of the decline of water were left without work (farmworkers.org, accessed February 2011).

The Mexican workers were most likely to be found working on the railway, in the mines, or in the agricultural sector. Because of their immigrant status, they were exploited more than their Anglo migrant counterparts, and wages were extremely low.

Mexican workers freely labored throughout the U.S. workforce with governmental support until 1924, when the Border Patrol was formed. At this point, Mexican workers were no longer welcomed as needed laborers in various work sectors, but instead became "illegal" fugitives "obliging them to live in hiding so that they will not be arrested and deported" (ibid.). This point in the history of migration was crucial, for it was at this time that employers no longer needed to operate with governmental work contracts if their employees were living and working in the United States illegally. Therefore, contract work in unison with debt bondage became characteristic of the Mexican migrating class. Because their labor could be secured for little to no pay (depending on any existing debts to the employer), Mexican workers became the primary migrant class; they remain so today, as is illustrated in the case study of Immokalee.

Agricultural slavery is widespread throughout the United States. In fact, the Coalition of Immokalee Workers estimates that at any one time, approximately 5 percent of U.S. farmworkers are subjected to forced labor (ciw-online.org, accessed May, 2011). However, due to the invisibility of agricultural slaves, the number is arguably much higher than the CIW estimates. Mirroring the historical evolution of slavery, the majority of those trapped in debt bondage are of Mexican descent, although the United States is experiencing an influx of Guatemalan and Haitian agricultural laborers. Earning less than $10,000 a year, with no benefits, agricultural laborers are forced to work in horrific and dangerous conditions, unable to alter their life situation because of an insurmountable debt accrued through their migration. Due to their undocumented status, the workers are not able make demands to their employers, nor are they able to report their slavery.

Immokalee is not unique in its being a hub for agricultural slavery, for this form of forced labor is evident in all corners of the United States. From the tomato pickers in Florida to the strawberry harvesters in California, no agricultural community is completely immune from the possibility that the migrant laborers, especially those who are undocumented, are forced to work in slave-like conditions. Agricultural slaves have been identified in small apple orchards in Illinois, as well as Christmas tree fields in the Northeast. As long as there is a demand for cheap labor, as well as a vulnerable undocumented migrating population, agricultural slavery will persist in the United States.

Because Immokalee is not unique, and because agricultural slavery is not confined to this single case, the patterns that I have unearthed in Immokalee are also not exclusive, for the patterns associated with agricultural slavery in Immokalee are apparent in other communities in which this form of forced labor has been identified. For example, as already noted, the country of origin for identified agricultural slaves is most likely to be Mexico, Guatemala, or Haiti. However, agricultural slaves may be trafficked from anywhere in the world, including within the United States. Unfortunately, while advocates and law enforcement are more likely to identify workers who appear undocumented as working in slave-like conditions, farmworkers in general are vulnerable to slavery and debt bondage.

Beyond the immigration status of identified slaves, the general experiences of those trapped in slavery are similar throughout the country. In the majority of identified cases in the United States:

> an element of debt bondage is involved. Traffickers promise to take workers on credit to well-paid jobs where the debt incurred for transport can be paid off quickly. In some instances, workers arrive at the place of work already thousands of dollars in debt. Subsequently they are forced to pay off their debts in conditions to which they did not agree, working in the fields for 12-14 hours a day, seven days a week. Deductions are made from their wages for transport, accommodation, food, work equipment, and supposed tax and social security payments. Weekly wages are sporadic and in many instances workers are left with no pay (Antislavery International 2011).

In addition:

> Workers are coerced in a number of ways and the violent treatment of victims can be extremely traumatic. Enslaved workers are taken to labor camps where they face brutality and a near-total loss of control over their lives. As many as 12-16 pickers may be housed in one cramped, run-down trailer, kept under constant surveillance by employers using a variety of methods, including armed guards. Some endure a constant barrage of verbal abuse along with threats of violence and death to themselves and their families back home. In the most severe cases, employers use public beatings, pistol-whippings, and shootings to make an example of those trying to escape (ibid).

In spite of the atrocities related to modern agricultural slavery, there are some lessons that can be learned from the Immokalee example. The first is the strong element of external protection so evident in Immokalee. As highlighted in this chapter, workers who have external alliances, such as the CIW, are able to afford some "luxuries" associated with life improvements including a "penny-more-per-pound." Beyond the economic benefits, advocacy-based groups offer external support and protection, which serves as a liaison between the worker and the general public, thereby creating a system of social pressure against the farmers' compliance to modern-day slavery. Although not able to completely eradicate slavery, the external networks offer the farmworker the opportunity for improved work and life conditions. The actions and efforts of groups such as the CIW can provide the foundation for the development of other farmworker organizations that may benefit from the privileged status of the volunteers to draw national attention to the plight of the workers in their community. This in turn will allow for an increased recognition of agricultural slavery evident throughout the United States, as well as force improvements for farmworkers associated with the external network.

Beyond the development of farmworker advocacy organizations, after reading this chapter, readers are now more aware of the general indicators among the migrant class trapped in agricultural slavery. Lack of identification, the inability to leave a job, constant surveillance by field bosses, and the inability to speak for oneself are strong indicators associated with victims of agricultural slavery and human trafficking. Readers may also be more aware of the fresh produce available in their own community, yet they may still be unaware of where the produce is harvested. Perhaps upon deeper investigation, readers may identify agricultural slavery in fields on the outskirts of their own town. As highlighted in this chapter, entering Immokalee for the first time, an outsider would not be aware of the slavery associated with the tomato industry, for the evidence of forced labor is miles outside of the center of town. Attentiveness to these indicators will assist more and more members of the general public in identifying victims of agricultural slavery and reporting suspicions to the properly trained authorities. This chapter serves not only to identify agricultural slavery in Immokalee, but also to illuminate the reality of trafficking for purposes of forced labor throughout the United States. With the general similarities of victims of trafficking and agricultural slavery, this chapter provides the reader with the basic indicators and warnings that slavery is not an issue of the past or of another country, but rather is evident in farming communities throughout the United States.

Although agricultural slavery is arguably a horrific reality that is difficult to acknowledge as happening in our own backyard, this form of slavery is not the only type evident in Immokalee or in the United States. Immokalee is not recognized as a microcosm of modern-day slavery merely for the evidence of agricultural slavery. As noted in the introduction to this book, in addition to agricultural slavery, domestic servitude and trafficking for purposes of sexual exploitation have also been identified in Immokalee. The following chapter opens the closed doors of dilapidated shacks to highlight the experiences of the women and children who have been trafficked across the borders and forced into the much-in-demand commercial sex industry in Immokalee, Florida.

---

[1] This information was based on information obtained in arrest reports regarding occupation and place of birth

[2] Domhoff worked within a typology of power based on ideology, political, military, and economic criteria.

[3] Information derived from interviews, as well as the CIW's *Facts and Figures of Farmworkers.*

3

Forced Commercial Sex Labor

"Caged birds sing of freedom, free birds fly."
—Thorolf Rafto

In November 2009 I met with the assistant US district attorney of southern Florida who had prosecuted a number of slavery cases. He told me the following story that, for me, put the reality of forced commercial sex labor in perspective. A very powerful member of the Guatemalan elite had decided to move to the United States with his wife and family. Before he left Guatemala, he felt it necessary to take a young girl, against her will, who was to work as an indentured servant for his family, as well as be his own personal sex slave. He did not hide this kidnapping from Guatemalan officials, for he was aware that with his level of power, no one would challenge him—and no one did. He successfully brought the girl to the United States. For the next few years, the young girl was forced to work as a nanny and housekeeper for the "lady of the house," in addition to her enduring constant sexual assault by her kidnapper. Often he would share her with his close friends and other relatives as a gift, or for a small fee; daily, she was passed from man to man. The activities remained hidden behind the massive walls of an upper-class southern Florida neighborhood for years.

At first, the wife did not seem to mind exploiting the young girl's free domestic labor. In fact, it was her own personal luxury to have a private nanny and housekeeper. Eventually the husband's constant sexual attention toward the young girl aroused the wife's intense jealousy, which led to a number of domestic disputes. Neighbors said nothing despite the constant quarrelling that could be heard through open windows, until one evening, the shouts gave way to physical violence. At this point, the neighbors thought it was important to bring the disputes to the attention of the local police. When the police arrived, after an investigation of the home, they found the young girl on a dirty mattress on the floor in a room with no other furniture. Surprised by her presence, the responding officers asked the girl who she was, to which she responded, "I am the slave." The assistant US district attorney was successful in his prosecution, as the husband/defendant was sentenced to 168 months of imprisonment and 3 years of supervisory release in 2000 (*United States v. Tecum*, 2001).

Beyond the realm of everyday consciousness, yet readily available to be sensationalized by media outlets, forced commercial sex labor exists throughout the United States; everywhere from the dark, decrepit corners of makeshift brothels to behind the walls that are obscured by wealth and power. There is no space that is immune to the cycle of rape and abuse that vulnerably marginalized women and children consistently endure. The purpose of this chapter is not to further feed the sensationalism of the experiences of the women and children trapped in forced commercial sex labor, but rather to identify why this industry continues to persist, as well as to discuss the general experiences and indicators associated with forced commercial sex labor in Immokalee. This chapter will be divided into six sections. I will begin by discussing a brief history of commercial sex trafficking in the United States. This will be followed with an analysis of the distinct attributes associated with sex trafficking in comparison to prostitution and other forms of human trafficking in Immokalee. I will then turn the attention of the chapter to the specific attributes associated with sex trafficking in Immokalee, beginning with the generalities related to the women and children trafficked into Immokalee for purposes of sexual exploitation and proceeding to an examination of the distinct types of sex trafficking evident in Immokalee. Finally, I will conclude the chapter with a discussion of the continuous demand for sex trafficking, as well as the individual consequences associated with those trapped in sex trafficking. As with the agricultural slave laborers in Immokalee, this is only one of many sex trafficking cases in the United States. However, the experiences are real, and the lessons we can take by analyzing one case can lead to a deeper understanding of sex trafficking nationwide.

The data collected regarding foced commercial sex labor is not easily obtained due to its hidden nature. Therefore, the data collected for this chapter was gathered through street-level observations. These observations were made possible through the assistance of by local police, detectives, and advocates.

From White Slavery to Sex Trafficking

Although this slavery in its various forms has existed throughout history, the discussion of women and children as victims of the sex trade has its roots in the end of the nineteenth century into the beginning of the twentieth century. Known then as "white slavery," the practice referred to the "procurement—by use of force, deceit or drugs—of a white woman or girl against her will for prostitution" (Kangaspunta 2010: 1). Early estimates of women trafficked for purposes of sexual exploitation ranged from a handful upward into the hundreds:

> [S]ome figures show that trade in women did not exist in the end of 1800 and beginning of 1900. In 1912, police in Hamburg listed 402 known traders in women and identified another 644 in Eastern Europe. The US Immigration Bureau investigated traffic in women in London, Berlin, and Hamburg and identified 578 individuals involved in the trade (ibid.: 1).

The numbers, whatever the estimates, remained inaccurate and extremely low, for the discussion of trafficking for the purpose of sexual exploitation completely ignored non-White women. Eventually critics persuaded the lawmakers and advocates to identify the array of victims sold into the sex slave trade, and began to use the general term "human trafficking" (ibid.). Today, this term "is generally associated with the coercion of women and children (including male children) for the purposes of sexual exploitation and sexual gratification," and the global estimates of victims and perpetrators within the United States are annually in the tens of thousands (the term "human trafficking" encompasses all forms of forced labor, but is generally misunderstood to include only the forced commercial sex industry).

Forced Commercial Sexual Labor Versus Agricultural Slavery in Immokalee

Before examining human trafficking for purposes of sexual exploitation in Immokalee, it is important to address distinct attributes associated with commercial sexual exploitation as compared to agricultural slavery in that community. The first of these is the criminalization versus victimization dichotomy. In Immokalee, women and children who have been identified in the forced commercial sex industry are more easily accepted as victims of trafficking, whereas the field workers discussed in Chapter 2 are initially treated as a criminal due to their undocumented labor status. In other words, the field workers must prove their victimization by providing information regarding forced labor, as well as other indicators of slavery (economic abuse, physical confinement, etc.). Women and children need not prove their victimization, for the evidence is forthright (e.g., confinement or the identification of a working brothel). This dichotomy of victimization versus criminalization refers to the coercive nature related to the forced commercial sex industry. Agricultural migrants are more likely to be viewed as voluntarily entering the United States in search for work; therefore the more pressing issue of the abusive work conditions is often overlooked.

The dichotomy of victimization and criminalization is not exclusive to Immokalee; it is evident throughout the literature, as well as the domestic laws regarding human trafficking. For example, section 102 (a) of the Trafficking in Persons Protection Act states as the purpose of the law "to combat trafficking in persons, a contemporary manifestation of slavery whose victims are predominantly women and children, to ensure just and effective punishment of traffickers, and to protect their victims" (2000). Granted, section 102 (b)(3) does highlight that "[t]rafficking in persons is not limited to the sex industry. This growing transnational crime also includes forced labor and involves significant violations of labor, public health, and human rights standards worldwide" (ibid.). However, the key components of the Act refer more specifically to women and children. In terms of definitional issues, the definition as posited by the United Nations specifically includes "the exploitation of the prostitution of others or other forms of sexual exploitation, *forced labour or services, slavery or practices similar to slavery, servitude* or the removal of organs" (UNDOC; italics added) as the various forms of human trafficking. However, media sources paint an image of forced commercial sex labor as the sole source of modern-day slavery. The core reason for the attention differential to various forms of trafficking is the fact that the trafficking of women and children is the most publicized form of trafficking worldwide, partly due to the social innocence and image of moral purity associated with women and children. In other words, socially, women and children are deemed to require more protection, and therefore their status of morally innocent victim accentuates the publicity of sex trafficking when victimization has been identified. Aside from the media frenzy associated with the identification of women and children forced into commercial sex labor, moral crusaders have emphasized the importance of protecting the sexual morality of young women and children and have been influential in policy change and implementation.

Related to the victimization/criminalization dichotomy is the legal distinction between sex trafficking and prostitution. Legally, prostitution is not only deemed a voluntary act worthy of criminalization, but there also exists an underlying motive to curb illegal immigration. Only those undocumented immigrants who are recognized as "victims of severe forms of trafficking" will receive the benefits of "visas and work permits, welfare support, and even the possibility of permanent residency" (Chapkis 2003: 924). Because of the assumed voluntary nature of prostitution, abuse and exploitation are considered to be unfortunate realities, but not worthy of federal protection. However, the majority of women in all arenas of the sex industry enter under false pretenses; they are physically and psychologically abused, isolated, and denied the freedom of movement. Therefore, in order to fully understand the sex industry in Immokalee, prostitution is not separated in this discussion from trafficking insofar as both are controlling and involuntary.

Aside from the criminalization versus victimization dichotomy, other attributes also exist that distinguish commercial sexual exploitation from agricultural forced labor. The first of these is the obvious gender differential. Practically all of the identified victims of sex trafficking in Immokalee have been women. This not to say that young boys cannot be trafficked into the world of forced commercial sex labor, but it is rare. In fact, according to one advocate interviewed, only one boy had been identified as a victim of sex trafficking in the last five years. And never in Immokalee has a man over the age of eighteen been identified. Perhaps the young boys who are trafficked for sexual purposes are not as easily identified as such because of the assumption that this is a crime that only affects young women. We as a society are more likely to be suspicious and protective of young women who could be potential victims, thereby overlooking the possibility that a young boy could be experiencing the same torturous conditions. Whatever the reason may be, in terms of those who have been identified as victims, sex trafficking is gendered.

The age of those trafficked for sexual purposes is the second distinctive attribute. Although the terms "women" and "girls" are generally used interchangeably, the majority of those trafficked into the United States are under the age of eighteen. Legally, the young women under eighteen are the primary victims that officials seek to identify and protect. A trafficked woman over that age has a much more difficult time proving her coercion into involuntary sexual services. In other words, a woman over the age of eighteen performing sexual acts for money is rarely deemed a victim of trafficking, but rather a prostitute by choice. This proves to be a difficult dilemma in that a woman over eighteen may be trafficked into the United States, but in order to escape her bondage, she has the overwhelming task of proving that her victimization is not an aspect of profession. More importantly, if she is identified as a victim, she will not receive legal protection or the benefits proffered by advocacy groups unless she agrees to assist in the prosecution of the trafficker. A young woman under the age of consent is guaranteed legal protection if she is identified as a victim of sex trafficking, even if she refuses to assist in the prosecution of the trafficker. Therefore, the majority of those who have been identified and rescued from a system of sex bondage have found to be under eighteen.

Another distinct attribute of the forced commercial sex industry is its invisibility. Many of the farmworkers are visible in Immokalee after work hours; it is not uncommon to see them riding their bikes through town or sitting outside with friends and/or family. On Friday nights, the streets are crowded with farmworkers looking for activities to relieve themselves from the stress of the brutal work week in the fields. Of course, as mentioned earlier, these laborers are not as visible at work, due to the hidden location and secure environment of the fields. Yet, once the shift is over, workers are easily identified as they climb off the work buses in the center of town and convene with acquaintances well into the evening.

The women and children trapped in a system of sexual slavery are not as obviously visible as the meandering farmworkers, for they are usually kept somewhere so as not to draw attention to their bondage. In those rare instances when the trafficked girl is out in public, she blends into the community landscape so well that only upon approaching her and asking of her situation would one become aware that she is trapped in sexual slavery. The trafficker is aware that a young child dressed provocatively would draw the attention of the authorities and advocates. She therefore is usually modestly clothed, appearing no different from all the other young children in the community. Many of the buyers of young girls are fulfilling a pedophilic fantasy, so her appearance of an innocent child serves the double purpose of hiding her situation and appealing to potential buyers. On the other hand, women trapped in sexual slavery are many times identified in terms of their criminal status as prostitutes. Therefore, their provocative dress and demeanor is considered as part of the profession. These women are more likely to be questioned in terms of their criminality rather than their victimization associated with trafficking. As one local officer commented, "We are more concerned with the young girls, because women over the age of eighteen are not forced [to be prostitutes]." Again, this mindset reaffirms the general social distinction between prostitution and human trafficking without recognition of the overlap.

Although some of the young children trafficked for purposes of sexual exploitation are allowed to be in public, in general these child victims, as well as women forced into prostitution, remain socially invisible. The social invisibility of the women and children is practical for two reasons: victim identification and restraint. In terms of identification, due to the established victimized status of women and children who have been trafficked for purposes of sexual exploitation, as previously noted, young women who appear to be victims of sex trafficking are more likely to be approached by advocates and/or local law enforcement. This, in turn, creates an outlet of escape if the young women believe there is a safety net of protection from the trafficker.

The practical invisibility of the young women is also a product of the psychological restraint. Many of the young women arrive to the United States only knowing one person: their trafficker. The trafficker employs not only the same psychological tactics that are used on the farmworkers (e.g., physical threats to the victim as well as to her family), but also strategies that lead the victim to truly believe that she is *owned* by her trafficker. For example, according to information developed in the prosecution of a local trafficker, one young girl was enslaved by the mere perception that her trafficker owned her soul because he carried a lock of her hair in a necklace. Based on her religious beliefs, because he had a piece of her body, he also had a piece of her soul. He carried this with him at all times as a reminder to her that she belonged to him. When he was arrested, the piece of hair was found on his body and assisted in corroborating the young girl's story of her victimization (*United States v. Tecum* 2001). Because he owned her body and soul, he was able to hold her captive in his basement with full knowledge that she would not attempt to escape. There was no need for chains or locks.

Many of the young women are invisible simply because they are physically restrained from leaving their living quarters, unless they are accompanied by a relative or acquaintance of the trafficker. When in public, as earlier stated, the victim appears to be an ordinary child who is accompanied by an adult to church, the store, or even school. She may be presented as a domestic servant or nanny, or as a distant relative (e.g., a niece). Because there is the illusion of freedom, no one really questions her status or situation. However, when at home, many of the young women are chained to walls or locked in small rooms to thwart escape. There have been cases where a girl was found in a basement with no windows. The walls were concrete so that no sunlight came in, and no screams went out. She was silenced and invisible. In another case, although the girl was allowed to serve guests as a domestic servant, she was kept in a broom closet when she was not needed. The young woman becomes hidden in plain sight, in that she may be escorted through the town by a respectable member of society, or serves guests in the home so as to be deemed a caretaker for the family rather than a sex slave. Many times, after the fact, friends and neighbors are appalled to learn that right across the street a young girl was forcibly being passed around as a sexual object behind closed doors of suburban America.

The final attribute distinguishing those trafficked into forced commercial sex labor from those trafficked into forced agricultural labor is the mode of recruitment. As discussed in the previous chapter, many of the men trafficked are aware that they will find work in the agricultural sector. The system of coercion occurs when these migrant workers reach the United States and find that they have an insurmountable debt to repay and no avenue of escape. In other words, many of the migrant workers are smuggled into the United States, and their trafficking begins when the trafficker confiscates identification and demands debt repayment. On the other hand, a larger majority of young women trafficked into the United States arrive here believing that they will be employed as domestic servants, usually as a nanny or housekeeper. It is a fair assumption to believe that the young girls trafficked into the United States do not choose to do so with the complete understanding and desire that they will become prostitutes. In other words, rarely will an identified victim state that she wanted to be a prostitute, let alone a sex slave. As illustrated in the introduction to this book, chances are that she will be confronted in her own country by a trustworthy woman (who is in fact the trafficker) and told that a family in the United States needs to fill a nanny position because this older woman has retired and moved back to her country of origin. The young woman feels comforted by this older woman and her stories of all the promises the United States has to offer, and agrees to take over the domestic duties. Immediately upon arrival, the young girl's identification papers are confiscated by the trafficker, and she is told she must repay her travel costs before she can regain her papers. She is then taken to a home or brothel and forced to perform sexual acts until her debt (upwards of $10,000) is paid.

Interestingly, as a local detective shared with me, sometimes when the women and/or children are identified, they may refuse acknowledging their victimization. For example, in one case about which I was told, a young girl was identified working in a brothel. She was offered to have her debt repaid to the trafficker in return for her assistance in the arrest and subsequent prosecution of her trafficker. She refused the offer. Instead, she explained that she was so close to repaying her debt that she would continue to do so in return for her freedom from her trafficker. In other words, a debt of approximately $10,000 had almost been repaid through her forced sexual services, of which she received approximately $30 from each buyer. The victim had worked for such a long period of time that she believed she could earn her freedom through just a few more sexual services. Although there was an obvious psychological restraint by the trafficker, most likely through threats to her and her family, she no longer saw herself as a victim.

Other young women do not even have an opportunity to make the decision to come to the United States (under false pretenses). This group of young women is actually sold to the traffickers by family members. Parents buy into the illusion of freedom and opportunity that could only benefit their daughter, and so they sell her to the traffickers. Although parents may profit from the sale, they do so thinking that the transaction is more about giving their daughter an opportunity and chance that they could not otherwise offer her. In rarer occurrences, some women are utilized as a form of debt repayment by their partners who are already trapped in agricultural slavery. Although this scenario is not identified as often, it has been the case that a male partner is offered the opportunity to decrease his debt in trade for the sexual services of his wife or girlfriend. She may or may not have her own debt to repay, but in either case, she is now forced to work to relieve her husband's debt. She is rarely identified as a victim of human trafficking because of what appears to be her voluntary choice to work as a prostitute, and therefore she has limited opportunities to escape and benefit from legal and social protections.

The traffickers are so perfectly camouflaged within the American landscape that to detect a perpetrator is virtually impossible without the assistance of an identified victim. However, successful prosecutions of traffickers have revealed indicators as well as the organizational structure of the trafficking "enterprise." In general, "organized businesses and crime networks...were instrumental in recruiting...women" (Raymond and Hughes 2001: 7). Internationally connected street gangs have also entered into the business of human trafficking. Overall, human trafficking is a business, and a quite profitable one. Millions of dollars are to be made through debt bondage, as well as through the buyers of the women and the sexual services.

Because many of the ringleaders have a history of criminal activity, the money is easily concealed to avoid detection.

Aside from hiding the money trail, most trafficking organizations are laterally structured. In other words, there is no single leader, but rather a network of leaders who display equitable levels of immense power. These leaders are the puppet masters of the trafficking organization, and are virtually impossible to identify. Beyond the leaders are many layers of people who move and guard the women, as well as sell the women to sex businesses and private buyers. It is the lower-level workers that are the first to be identified and prosecuted. This decentralized structure is fundamental to maintaining the organization, for the lower-level players are easily replaced (usually recruited from the same population as the trafficked victims). More importantly, the layers allow for a relationship between the workers and leaders, yet if leaders are identified, the leaders are able to hide behind invisible deniability. This deniability is equivalent to the relationship between the farmers and farm bosses discussed in Chapter 2.

In Immokalee, prosecutions relating to the trafficking of women and children for purposes of sexual exploitation have involved the low-level traffickers and the private buyers of the women and children. This is partly because the women are unlikely to have contact with the trafficking leaders. Therefore, they are only to identify those who have moved them and/or those who have confined them in Immokalee. Advocates have emphasized the organized nature of human trafficking and express that the only true way to eradicate trafficking is to identify and punish the leading offenders. Because of the decentralized structure and hidden nature of the leaders of trafficking rings, the eradication of the trafficking enterprise is unlikely.

Sexual Slavery in Immokalee

In Immokalee, there are three main types of sexual slavery: prostitution in brothels, exotic dance clubs, and individual sex slaves belonging to a private citizen. The type of sexual slavery in which a woman finds herself is typically dependent on her age, her debt, and the trafficker. The younger women attract the pedophilic base of buyers, as well as the younger migrant workers, and are therefore more likely to be identified in brothels or confined in the home of an independent buyer. The women over the age of eighteen are more likely to be found in the dance clubs. With respect to debt, those with a greater amount of money owed are more likely to be paying their debt through prostitution, or a buyer has paid the woman's debt, but in return, she belongs to him. Those with little to no debt may be trafficked into Immokalee and found in the dance clubs. It is the trafficker who has the final say as to where the trafficked women will work, and so, depending on his/her obligated territory, it is most likely that the trafficked women will be placed where the trafficker believes it will be most profitable and carry less risk of identification. Consequently, the women trafficked into Immokalee for purposes of sexual exploitation have no say in where they will be found, for the location of work is dependent on factors beyond their control.

The Brothels

A dilapidated building, hidden behind walls of weeds and bamboo, is a suspected brothel under investigation this evening. Sitting in an unmarked vehicle, we quietly watch through binoculars to see if any activity will occur on this Friday night. Local police had told me that this particular building has been thought to be a brothel, but up to this time, there has been no clear evidence to support the assumption. On this evening however, the police are fairly confident that activities will take place, and so we sit and observe to see if the police can get any closer to closing down another brothel in Immokalee.

There are a number of indicators to determine if a working brothel is in existence. The first is whether or not there appears to be a clear attempt to hide the building. Although many of the homes in Immokalee have overgrown plants and unkempt yards, the "green" walls utilized to hide the building are purposeful. Bamboo growing thickly around the boundaries of the property is an obvious form of concealment. Other brothels may have a newly crafted privacy fence, or a padlocked chain-link fence. Finally, some brothels are chosen because the building was built with limited visibility from the road, and therefore are naturally secreted from the prying passer-by. The building under investigation that Friday evening exhibited all of the landmark indicators of secrecy. It had bamboo growing wildly around the back of the building. Around the front was a crudely constructed chain-link fence that at this time was open for potential buyers. The building was also set so far back from the main road that it was easily overlooked by those driving by.

Aside from the attempt to conceal a building, the actual building itself is another indicator the existence of a brothel. Some brothels seem to pop up overnight, as they are simply old trailers or prefabricated sheds sitting in what was once an empty lot. These brothels require strict observation on the part of the local advocates and police, for many times the sheds and trailers merely melt into the Immokalee landscape. Other brothels are formed in abandoned homes. If a trafficker is able to find an abandoned home, it is much less risky for him to run the brothel. The home is ideally boarded up, the landscape is most likely overgrown, creating the secluding green curtain, and there is no reason to investigate as the home has been there for some time, rather than just showing up overnight. To find an abandoned home is superlative for the trafficker, but is not always likely. Therefore, many traffickers will rent a location under an assumed name and conduct the brothel activities out of the rented facility. The rented facilities are the most difficult to identify in that they are usually kept by a landlord and the indicators are less obvious.

Once inside the brothel, the interiors are disturbingly similar. A brothel that had just been discovered was described as being similar to the many other brothels previously identified in Immokalee. The floors were old wooden slats, so rotten that one officer's foot crashed through a floorboard. There were three main rooms: a waiting room and two bedrooms. The waiting room had a number of folding chairs, a couch, and a television to keep the waiting buyers occupied. While the police were investigating this particular brothel, they were sickeningly disturbed by the images of a popular animated underwater character being viewed on the television.

The bedrooms were identical. Each had an old mattress on the floor, stained with ineradicable bodily fluids. Over the windows were moth-eaten sheets acting as curtains yet allowing for very little privacy. There were no other furnishings in the room with the exception of a candle. As was told to me, a large majority of the brothels that have been identified had the candle of Santa Muerte in the bedrooms. Santa Muerte, or the Death Saint, is known as the Mexican protector of souls of the underworld, and she is most often found among the Mexican underclass and criminal organizations. In terms of her relation to criminal groups, including prostitutes, she is asked to protect from criminal detection. Some of the advocates I spoke with believe that the women trapped in the brothels find security in the presence of Santa Muerte as they pray to her for protection.

The brothels are a depressing and unsanitary sight, yet this does not deter the buyers. In fact, the suspected brothel that we were observing had over seven visitors within an hour. They would park their bikes against the porch of the building, and enter the home without knocking. Within minutes, they would return to their bikes and travel back to the center of town as if this was part of their scheduled business for the day. To any naive passer-by, the exchange could just as easily have been friends just checking in with each other, for each patron stayed for such a short time, and showed no indication of change in behavior, so that the entire event was completely unassuming. Buyers have a number of means to find the location of the otherwise secret brothel. Sometimes a buyer will learn of the location through word of mouth. This is the most difficult situation for local police, for there is no way to overhear this information without a trustworthy informant. Because of this, the police often rely on other forms of "advertising."

The most popular form of advertising a brothel is through party fliers. In order not to confuse a traditional party flier with a brothel advertisement, the police focus on the time frame for the "party" rather than the actual information on the flier, for most of the information is identical to a typical dance party advertisement. If the party begins in the early evening (e.g., 5:00) and concludes within a few hours, this is an indicator that the advertisement could be a cover for prostitution, and the location of the brothel is clearly written for the buyer who has an understanding of the code. In some cases, the advertisement will also include a map to the location. Although the flier is not a clear indicator of a working brothel, it is a starting point for local police as they attempt to uncover a new location. After a flier is found, investigators will drive by or surveil the advertised location and look for other indicators of a working brothel, such as men entering and leaving the location after staying only for short periods of time, as well as attempts to conceal the location with walls, fences, and other forms of camouflage. If indicators are present, officers may further the investigation to determine whether and what sort of illegal activity is occurring. Again, this is not an explicit sign that a brothel is being operated, but it is a starting point in uncovering what would otherwise have been a concealed location.

As for finding an advertisement, that is as easy as walking down the main street in Immokalee. Advertisements are handed out by lower-level workers of the traffickers, posted on street poles, or just tossed aside on the street as litter.

Exotic Dance Clubs

The brothels are not the only location of sexual exploitation in Immokalee. As stated earlier, many of the young women trafficked for purposes of sexual exploitation are found in exotic dance clubs. Although the girls are brought in as dancers, many times the stripping is forced, tips are given to traffickers, and in a number of cases, many of the buyers expected prostitution. The locations of the clubs vary from side-street buildings to moving vehicles, although most of the clubs serve the primary purpose of being a bar. The word is used quite liberally, for these are truly one-room buildings with the word BAR painted over the door.

The women that are trafficked into the strip clubs are distinct from the girls found in the brothels in that most are actually trafficked to Immokalee from within the United States, usually from larger metropolises such as Miami and Tampa. As stated earlier, these women may be a little older than the girls found in the brothels, yet the coercive and controlling nature of trafficking remains evident. In rare cases, minor girls will be brought into the clubs to dance, depending on the interests of the clientele, but this is not as common as in the brothels. Although the experience of the dancers may not be the same, many of the women were trafficked into the United States years ago. At that time, it was most likely that they would work in brothels in the city in which they initially arrived. The reasons vary as to why some of the women are eventually trafficked to Immokalee, including but not limited to financial gain to the trafficker, the "aging out" of the woman from brothel work, or sale of the girl to another trafficker in Immokalee. Once she arrives in Immokalee, she is forced to dance in the clubs and is under constant surveillance by the trafficker.

The women being forced to strip and engage in prostitution in Immokalee is a relatively new phenomenon, or at least it has just recently come to the attention of the local law enforcement. Because of the age of the dancers, as well as the seemingly voluntary nature of the prostitution, the women in the clubs have been identified as criminal rather than a victim of trafficking. Not until recently has it been exposed that these women are as victimized as all other victims of trafficking in Immokalee, despite their visibility and the nature of their work. Unfortunately, the identification of the dancer as a victim usually occurs after an arrest, and in many cases, she is too fearful to divulge her victimization to the local police. Therefore, the number of women trafficked into Immokalee and forced to strip and prostitute themselves is relatively unknown.

Independent Buyers

The third type of sexual exploitation evident in Immokalee is what I refer to as the girls for sale to independent buyers. The girls found in this type of trafficking situation are sold when they are extremely young, averaging around the age of thirteen. However, based on the "consumer demand," some girls are sold as young as four, while others are sold in their late teens. The sale of the girls usually occurs in a similar manner: family members selling to a trafficker, followed by the trafficker selling the girl to an independent buyer (usually a legal citizen). Other girls are discovered by the traffickers as runaways and then sold to an independent buyer. Finally, some girls are trafficked into the United States to work in the brothels, but are discovered by an independent buyer who offers to pay her debt, as was indicated in the introductory chapter scenario. Whatever the means of her sale, such a girl has absolutely no control over her purchase.

Once a girl has been bought, her situation is generalizably similar. Again, as with the other types of victims of trafficking, each victim will endure her own unique experience, but victims who have been identified share a familiar set of commonalities; these include their responsibilities to their "owner," their living conditions, and their treatment before discovery. Many of the girls are bought by men who have wives and families. Therefore, one of the responsibilities for the girl will to be provide household services such as cleaning, and if plausible, working as a nanny for younger children. This set of responsibilities not only provides a service to the family, but it also affords to disguise the actual reasons for the girl to be living in the home. This disguise becomes especially important when visitors arrive at the home and notice the new girl living with the family. The mirage of domestic helps serves as a beneficial legal front, but behind closed doors, the young girl is considered to be nothing more than a sexual object for the buyer and anyone else he deems worthy of using her. Many times, she is passed from man to man to man with no time for rest or recovery.

Aside from the constant sexual abuse, many of the girls who have been identified are found to be living in a similar type of living condition. To thwart any attempt of escape, the girls are usually chained to a wall or locked in a closet-size room, most often found in a basement. The girl is under constant surveillance by her "owner," as well as his family. She is not allowed to leave the home unless one of the family members acts as a chaperone. At times, she is pawned off on a neighbor, but she is most often seen in public with the buyer or a member of his family. In one case, a thirteen-year-old girl was taken by a neighbor to a local hospital because she was having complications with her pregnancy. No one questioned why a thirteen-year-old was pregnant, and she was returned to her trafficker with no further inquiry. This example illustrates that even in the rare instances when she is out of the home without being under surveillance of the family, her situation is clearly invisible to those who could potentially be of assistance.

Other girls are not physically imprisoned, but rather are psychologically restrained. As with all victims of trafficking, the buyers employ threats of death and/or deportation to keep the girl from escaping or reaching out for help. As stated earlier, other buyers have recourse to "magic," claiming to have taken the girl's soul, leaving her as his servant. When identified, the young girl has so often been raped, abused, and "caged" that she either displays symptoms of Stockholm syndrome or she is too fearful to talk to anyone outside of her enclosed world. Legally, once identified, because of her young age, she is still able to receive assistance from local advocates regardless of whether wants to speak out against her abuser.

Although young girls have been found in Immokalee as victims of human trafficking in the form of being sold to an independent buyer, this is considered to be the rarest type of sexual exploitation there. Interestingly, this type of trafficking has been discovered more often in the surrounding areas, including some of the most exclusive communities in southern Florida, yet the girls may be purchased from Immokalee. This is problematic in terms of identification and discovery in that these areas are not assumed to be conducive to trafficking for the purposes of sexual exploitation. However, as the next section will illustrate, the demand for sex trafficking is prevalent in every community.

Demand for Sexual Slavery

In the global context, "there are four components that make-up the demand: 1) the men who buy commercial sex acts, 2) the exploiters who make up the sex industry, 3) the states that are destination countries, and 4) the culture that tolerates or promotes sexual exploitation" (Hughes 2005: 7). Studies have dispelled the traditional myth of the lonely male buyer looking for an evening of companionship and instead have uncovered that the majority of men who go to prostitutes for gratification are married, with families. As noted by Hughes, "They are seeking control and sex in contexts in which they are not required to be polite or nice, and where they can humiliate, degrade, and hurt the woman or child, if they want" (ibid.). Men who buy sex from trafficked women and children are not seeking relationships; rather, they are fulfilling taboo fetishes (pedophilia and/or nonconsensual violence) with little to no consequence.

The buyers are not the only force in the demand for sexual slavery. Traffickers have learned that the trafficking of humans is much more profitable and continuous than, and involves little or no risk compared to, the trafficking of drugs or arms. Therefore, a number of arms dealers and drug traffickers have transferred their criminal expertise to the commodification and exploitation of women and children. Sex trafficking is the ideal business in that "the sexual services of trafficked victims can be sold again and again" (Yen 2008: 658). In other words, once a gun has been sold, the trafficker is unable to re-sell the same gun. However, a woman or child produces continuous profit, as she or he can be bought and sold multiple times any given day. "Indeed, global profits from sex trafficking are estimated to be between $7 and $12 billion dollars annually and growing rapidly" (ibid.: 659), which has resulted in the trafficking of humans being the most profitable criminal enterprise worldwide.

In addition to the high profit of sex trafficking is the limited penalty for the trafficker. Until recently, statewide and federal legislation regarding trafficking had limited penalties for offenders. In fact, "prior to the passing of the 2000 Trafficking of Victims Protection Act…the maximum statutory punishment for forcing someone to engage in involuntary servitude was only ten years" (ibid.). Even with the passing of the TVPA and various state laws, some violators have been sentenced to no more than six years. Therefore, "given its low investment costs, quick returns, very high profit margins, low risk of arrest, and relatively light penalties, sex trafficking has a very high profit-to-cost ratio among comparable criminal activities" (Yen 2008).

The demand for sex trafficking is not exclusive to buyers and exploiters, for destination states not only offer an economic dream easily utilized by traffickers, but also passively promote a culture of sexual consumption. Scholars have unequivocally argued that factors underlying sex trafficking include "an increase in poverty and unemployment in developing countries, the lack of educational and economic opportunities for women and the consequent feminization of poverty…" (ibid.: 657). These global crises have been useful tools of promise, for the destination countries are more and more likely to be in the first world and have been construed as locations of dream fulfillment and economic success. Therefore, it is easy for families and young girls to be influenced by the economic guarantees of the trafficker.

Not only is the economic image of the destination country a component in the demand for trafficking, but so is the consumption of sexuality itself in industrial nations. For example, "the Internet has played an important role in the construction of systems of communication between pedophile networks and between suppliers and consumers of other services" (Taylor and Jamieson 1999: 264). Through the utilization of the World Wide Web, as well as cable or satellite television, "sexual representation has been liberalized in most developed societies" (ibid.: 273). As sexuality and sexual representations become more accepted and part of the cultural mainstream, there is also an increase "in the demand for performers, and other key figures, in the sex programs and the development of a significant new labor market..." (ibid.: 274). In other words, as the culture legitimizes sexuality through popular representation and communication, the destination state passively partakes in the underground commodity exchange associated with sex trafficking.

Compared to the global demand for the sexual slave trade, the demand in Immokalee is quite similar, yet on a more secluded and smaller scale. There is a demand for sex from the men of Immokalee and surrounding areas. As noted earlier, many of the independent buyers of young girls are married with families and make use of the girls for their own pedophilic pleasure or for degradation and humiliation. On the other hand, many other buyers, such as those in the brothels or dance clubs, may not be married or have families; rather, they are seeking sex without a relationship responsibility. This search for personal pleasure with lack of respect for the woman and lack of responsibility was prevalent in the brothel under surveillance discussed earlier in the chapter. As we watched the men come and go from the brothel, we were able to determine that the average time spent in the brothel was seven minutes, leading to the conclusion that the buyers were not there to respect or develop a relationship with the girls, but rather to find sexual gratification with no responsibility and no constraints on what will lead to that gratification.

Similarly, the exploiters in Immokalee are making a great profit on the reusability of the women and children. In comparison with global and national human trafficking profits, the exploiters in Immokalee are not likely to achieve the incomes of the large-scale criminal enterprises. However, the traffickers in Immokalee are able to utilize the demand of the migrant population to generate high turnover rates on their low-priced investment. A victim in a brothel or dance club will generally be forced to perform sexual acts for multiple men in a single day, handing over the majority of the money that is earned back to the trafficker as debt repayment. As the debt becomes close to being paid off, another "cost" occurs, increasing the debt sometimes to the original fee. Therefore, the girls trafficked into sex work in the brothels and dance clubs generate a strong income for the traffickers.

As for the young girls that are sold to independent buyers, the traffickers are able to earn a price for the girl, as well as the cost of the "financial burden" of losing the business of the girl. Therefore, a young girl could generate well into the tens of thousands of dollars for the trafficker. Her buyer may then re-sell her to other interested pedophiles, creating a reusable profit for himself, in addition to the free labor that she may provide for his family. For the independent buyer, his family, and the brothel or club owners, the risk associated with sex trafficking is as minimal as it is on the national level. The relative invisibility of the victim, as well as misconceptions regarding sex trafficking and prostitution, have resulted in quite limited prosecutions of buyers, providing a similar low cost-to-risk ratio among those involved in the sex trafficking industry.

With respect to passive state complicity, the demand for sex trafficking in Immokalee is not immune to the cultural commodification of sexuality in the United States. Independent buyers can employ technology to communicate with trafficking rings, arranging the covert sale of young girls not readily available to legal identification. Additionally, the demand for sex without responsibility stems from a cultural objectification of young women. As discussed in the previous chapter, there exists a demand for cheap labor in the agricultural industry. At the same time, those who are forced into agricultural slavery have a demand for sexual gratification. Therefore, the demand for agricultural slavery breeds a demand for sex trafficking. In other words, because the migrants buy the services of the women in the brothels and clubs, they are maintaining the system of sexual slavery in Immokalee. Indirectly, because capitalism and consumerism have a need for cheap labor, the state is passively complicit in the continuance of the sex trade that is gratifying to the migrant workers in Immokalee. Even after the migrants leave the area, there still exists a base of buyers from the surrounding communities.

Consequences Experienced by Women and Children

The constant demand for sex trafficking has led to a number of consequences that the women and children must individually endure. Many of the consequences are obvious and inherent to the nature of sex trafficking, such as sexually related disease. The typical buyer believes that the woman must comply with his every demand, usually under the threat of physical violence if she does not, with one of the most popular requests being unprotected sex. As will be discussed in the next chapter, the spread of disease has become a concern of local advocates and police, and initiatives are being taken to promote safe sex practices. However, regardless of the education a young girl may gain, she is still alone in the room with the buyer, or under the complete control of her buyer, and due to the coercive and violent nature of trafficking, she must comply with his demands even if they push her to do exactly what advocates and police are attempting to prevent.

A second consequence to trafficking for purposes of sexual exploitation is pregnancy. The likelihood of pregnancy is quite high, and in some cases it is expected. As was highlighted by the case in the introductory section of the book, the birth of a child may be the sole reason for buying the girl. That young girl had been repeatedly raped, and had multiple pregnancies, all of which were aborted until she bore her owner a son. Other times the pregnancy is considered to be in the nature of the work, and she may either abort the child or choose to keep it. Many times the trafficker will force her to keep the child, for this offers him a new leverage of threat: "If you do not do what I ask you to do, I will kill your child." In the most extreme cases, the trafficker will exploit the child for additional income, selling the child to buyers with extremely young pedophilic desires. Although not as common in Immokalee, an advocate speaking out against trafficking at the national level informed me that a child at the age of three was sold in a nearby state. Therefore, if the demand exists, traffickers have the opportunity to exploit the child if the mother is allowed to keep her baby.

A girl becoming pregnant as a result of her trafficking could potentially lead to identification, and so a number of precautions are made so that if she does need to go to the hospital, she will not divulge herself as a victim. The trafficker will remind her of her undocumented status, threatening the possibility of deportation if she reveals herself. In addition, he will remind her that she is the prostitute and that information will be revealed to her family and friends if she exposes her own situation. Moreover, he will continue to make threats against her family in her country of origin. He will keep her identification, so that she has no way of proving her age or any other evidence that may validate her story. Lastly, he will threaten her economically, for she will not have insurance when she seeks medical services. Therefore, he will make her pay her medical expenses through her earnings, which in turn increases her debt to the trafficker. In sum, although the hospital or other medical facility provides an outreach to victims of trafficking, the overwhelming threat purported by the trafficker keeps the victim silent.

A less obvious consequence experienced by victims of sexual slavery is domestic violence. This is a unique phenomenon especially to those women who have been sold to the trafficker by their spouse. The abuse such a woman endures is so beyond her control that to escape the violence is relatively impossible. For example, a reason he may give her as to why he is abusing her is because she is "cheating on him," well aware that the reason for her prostitution is the paying off of his debt. Other times he may abuse her for not making the quota of money for the day. In a culture so permeated with *machismo*, many of the women are abused for the sole pretext of earning more than the spouse. As a method of control and display of dominance, he will reiterate that masculine power overrides economic gain. Over two years of observed arrest data in Immokalee, 18 percent of the arrests were battery/assault related, and a number of the battery/assault cases were recognized in police reports as domestic violence. Unfortunately, due to the undocumented status of the victims, a larger percentage of the acts of domestic violence go unreported (or victims will refuse to press charges), so an accurate account of how often domestic violence occurs in the Immokalee households is difficult to determine. Based on interviews, however, there is a common theme for outgoing calls involving domestic disputes, which has been theorized by advocates and police personnel in a number of cases to be related to the issues associated with trafficking, in particular sex trafficking.

It needs to be stated clearly that not all of the men forced into agricultural slavery in Immokalee sell their spouses to their trafficker, nor is it accurate to say that all of the men abuse their partners. However, in instances of abuse, there is a double oppression of sex and violence, leaving the woman with no avenue of escape. Even if her abuse is reported, it is likely that she will not press charges against her spouse, for her own status could be identified. Also, her fear of her trafficker is not relieved when she returns home, as the threats against herself and family are constant. Interestingly, domestic violence may be used as a tool by the trafficker, for he is aware that when she returns home she will have no means of escape. Even while she is not under the constant surveillance of her trafficker, the surveillance extends into her home. Therefore the consequence of domestic violence is a layer of abuse unique to those women who are allowed the freedom to return home, but only to an oppressive relationship.

Conclusion

Human trafficking for the purposes of sexual exploitation is a very real crime that is occurring in the very "back yard" across the American landscape. It is an offense that affects the most marginalized and vulnerable populations worldwide, yet it is often socially ignored, because to identify sexual slavery is to question our own responsibilities to the victims. Sexual slavery does exist, and it is the daily reality of thousands of women and children trafficked into the United States. In fact, it is estimated that 10,000 to 20,000 are trafficked annually into the United States, and that there are 30,000 to 50,000 sex slaves held in captivity in the United States at any given time (see Bales, freetheslaves.org).

Sexual slavery has been identified in all corners of the United States—urban, suburban, and rural. It has been identified in all forms, including, but not limited to, street prostitution, health clubs, strip clubs, escort services, and brothels. Major findings reveal that despite the form of sexual exploitation, there are a number of similarities among international women coerced into the sex industry in the United States (Raymond and Hughes, 2001). The first of these is the background of the women. Raymond and Hughes found that the majority of international women "entered the sex industry before the age of 25, many of them as children" (7) and most had "no or very little English language proficiency" (ibid.). Additionally, "[c]onditions facilitating recruitment of women include economic desperation and disadvantage, lack of a sustainable income, and poverty" (8). As with agricultural slavery, traffickers are able to exploit the oppressive conditions of poverty as a tool of recruitment.

Aside from the background of the women coerced into the sex industry, the experiences associated with sexual slavery, although unique to each woman and child, share common characteristics. The first of these is abuse. Raymond and Hughes found that violence, both psychological and physical, is intrinsically linked to the sex industry. Women are physically abused not only by traffickers, as a method of control, but also by buyers if they feel the women are not complying with their sexual requests. Women, as well as their families, are also verbally threatened. Most of the violence is unreported for reasons including "normalization or non-naming of the violence" (ibid.: 9).

Additional tactics of control include "denying freedom of movement, isolation, controlling money…intimidation, drug and alcohol addiction, threatened exposure of pornographic films, and sexual violence" (ibid.). Many of the women are kept under the constant eye of the trafficker, leaving any chance of escape impossible. Women in the sex industry have also reported that "economic necessity, drug dependencies and [traffickers] who beat them, kidnapped them, threatened them or their children prevented them from leaving" (ibid.: 10). Overall, regardless of the type of sex industry, the women (and children) identified suffer a reality of abuse with little to no chance of escape.

The women and children trapped in sexual slavery in Immokalee share a similar experience with their counterparts identified throughout the rest of the United States. They too are controlled through various types of abuse and verbal threats while being under the constant eye of the trafficker. Many of the women and children do not speak English, and all are forced to comply with the buyers' requests. They have been kidnapped or sold into the industry because of the oppressive poverty in their country of origin. The main difference between the women and children in Immokalee and the other international women in the sex industry throughout the United States is the country of origin. Raymond and Hughes found that the advertised nationality of women in the sex industry were predominantly Asian or Eastern European (ibid.). Although some were identified as Hispanic/Latina, in Immokalee the overwhelming majority of women and children trafficked for purposed of sexual exploitation are Hispanic/Latina. Most come from Mexico, while a growing number are being trafficked from Central and South America. A more recent phenomenon that is occurring is that women are now being domestically trafficked into Immokalee from Miami and other nearby metropolises.

Human trafficking for the purposes of sexual exploitation has its modern roots in white slavery, yet was identified early on by critics as a process that affects marginalized and vulnerable women and children worldwide. Poverty and lack of education, as well as global inequalities, have led to an increase of exploiters preying on the dreams and vulnerabilities of young girls and their families, forcing a system of forced prostitution and fostering pedophilia in the suburban landscape. Immokalee is not immune from the system of sexual slavery, nor is the case of this Florida community unique. In Immokalee, brothels are discovered behind walls of overgrown shrubbery or on vacant lots. Dance clubs house women forced to strip and perform sexual activities for demanding clients. Homes on the suburban cul-de-sacs house young girls forced to care for the home and/or children, while also experiencing repeated sexual assault by their "owner" and other clients. The hidden world of trafficking is flourishing in Immokalee, and the demand for the sexual experiences continues to increase. Meanwhile, the traffickers will continue to supply the demand as the profits are high and the risk is low.

Despite the overwhelming task of identifying cases of sexual slavery, for each case that is identified, a lesson is learned as to how we as a society can take measures to assist in the eradication of sexual slavery, while at the same time recognizing and protecting victims. The first, and perhaps most important, measure is to socially recognize the intersection between prostitution and sexual slavery. Regardless of immigration status, many prostitutes working domestically in the United States find themselves trapped in a trafficking situation. As noted, despite her immigration status, if she is under the age of eighteen, a girl is automatically regarded as a victim of trafficking due to the age of consent. The issue of prostitution versus trafficking becomes problematic when the victim is over eighteen. We cannot assume that in every case a woman in the sex industry has been coerced and is bonded to the situation. Rather, many women in the sex industry may define themselves as sex workers and voluntarily work as such. This is an uncertain area for activists and legal professionals in the identification and protection process, and therefore, women over eighteen need to be approached with respect and guaranteed the same protection as those under eighteen, whatever their level of volition is in the sex industry. In other words, we need to look beyond the profession and, without bias, make the determination whether the element of coercion is evident and whether someone else is making a profit off of the woman's exploitation.

In addition to the relationship between prostitution and sexual slavery, there are obvious indicators associated with trafficking that force public personnel to take responsibility for the victims and make the invisible visible. This is especially true for victims under eighteen, as well as undocumented women and children. The first indicator is someone else having control of the victim's identifying papers and money. As discussed earlier, many times the young girl will be taken to a hospital due to complications with her pregnancy, a termination of the pregnancy, the actual birth of a child, as well as sexually transmitted diseases. A clear sign of the victimization status of the young girl is if someone else hands any identification papers to the registering nurse and then takes the same identification papers to keep for himself; in other words, the proper identification of the young girl is never in her possession. In addition to the identifying papers, if the individual who accompanies the young girl to the hospital pays for her services in cash, this should alert some suspicion on the part of the registering nurse or accountant. Not only does this negate any paper trail, but if she is a victim of trafficking for purposes of sexual exploitation, she has now increased her debt to her trafficker. Taken together, these two acts alone are red flags for any medical professional coming into contact with a young girl who potentially is a victim of human trafficking.

Beyond identification papers and payment for medical services, those who come into contact with a possible victim should definitely be concerned if, in addition, the girl is well below the age of consent. In other words, medical professionals, as well as any other individual who may come into contact with the young girl (e.g., educators, neighbors, etc.), should ask why a thirteen-year-old is receiving medical attention for a pregnancy, or question why she repeatedly seeks treatment for sexually transmitted diseases. Of course, the pregnancy or sexually transmitted disease may not be the result of a trafficking situation, but it is the responsibility of those who have contact with such an individual to at least question her pregnancy and sexual relationships. Even if it is not a trafficking situation involving forced sexual intercourse, if the child is under eighteen, she is being exploited, as when being forced to strip in clubs. In short, if a member of the community comes into contact with a potential victim, rather than turning a blind eye, it is our responsibility to delve deeper into the situation and bring our suspicions to legal professionals and social advocates.

Not everyone will come into contact with a victim of trafficking for purposes of sexual exploitation, nor may they be aware that they are in contact with such a victim. Therefore, this chapter serves as a tool to assist in identifying areas that may be hubs for sexual trafficking. Because of the secrecy associated with private buyers of young girls, identifying a household that is keeping a young girl in captivity will be difficult for the everyday citizen. This identification is more accessible to neighbors, friends, and relatives who visit the inside of the home regularly. Therefore, everyday citizens may focus their attention on the public indicators of trafficking. The first is the appearance of a brothel. A building that appears to be vacant due to its neglected state, yet individuals come and go in brief intervals throughout the day, should be brought to the attention of the proper authorities. This is especially true if now and then a young girl is chaperoned in to the building and does not exit despite the number of men that are coming and going.

Brothels may not be as easily identified in large cities as in small close-knit communities. Therefore, a final location to question as to whether or not women and children are victims of trafficking for purposes of sexual exploitation is in the exotic dance clubs. Dance club enterprise owners have taken steps to eradicate trafficking in the clubs, which includes a basic education of the indicators as discussed in this chapter. Does the dancer have proper identification on her at all times, or does someone else hold her papers? What happens to her money? Does it go to someone else, possibly a person who surveils her as she works? Does someone speak for her? These indicators as well as her age and immigration status should be analyzed, and if there seems to be evidence of trafficking, authorities must be informed.

Although not evident in Immokalee, another location that is nationally a target of trafficking is the hotel industry. It has recently come to the attention of legal professionals and advocates that hotels are hot spots for advertising young girls to sell as "party favors" at various activities taking place at a hotel. One indicator as to whether or not a trafficking situation may be occurring, as with the dance clubs, is whether there is someone with the young girl who is obviously not a family member, yet has complete control of her money and identification. As this individual talks to the desk clerk, the young girl generally makes no eye contact. Another red flag associated with the hotel industry is a young girl checking into the hotel without luggage. Because of the newly recognized identification of the hotel industry as a demand center of sex trafficking, rather than prostitution, hotel employees are being trained by task forces across the country to assist in identifying those minor yet important details that are illustrative of a trafficking situation.

Human trafficking for purposes of sexual exploitation is widespread throughout the United States, yet the proprietors of the women and children are sure to keep the practices of sexual exploitation hidden from the public eye. The invisibility of sex trafficking has proven to be an effective tool in the maintenance of slavery, and an overwhelming obstacle for legal professionals and advocates alike. In spite of the seemingly impossible task of reducing the demand for both sexual slavery and agricultural slavery, there exist small groups that have the central mission of eradicating trafficking rings while protecting victims. Some of those involved in the anti-trafficking efforts are members of local law enforcement who have the difficult mission of identifying victims and prosecuting offenders, even while keeping open communication with the groups involved. On the other end of the spectrum, local advocates work to identify and protect victims of trafficking, while at the same time educating the public on the reality of human trafficking in the United States. Together, these groups have successfully assisted in the prosecution of a number of traffickers in Immokalee, and they continue in their efforts to educate and assist victims of human trafficking. The following chapters will identify a select few of these players in their attempts to eradicate human trafficking in Immokalee, while at the same time identifying and protecting victims despite their immigration status.

4

Law Enforcement Responses

> *"God loves everybody, and He doesn't draw those lines at…the Mexican
> and American border…"*
> —Anonymous

On a warm March afternoon, I pull my car into the small lot of the Immokalee substation, just off the main road into in town. It is an unassuming brick building with almost no cars parked in the lot. I am not quite sure if I am at the correct location, for I do not see a barrage of squad cars or high levels of security. The only indication that I have arrived at the correct location is the small sign that reads "District 8 Immokalee Substation." I park my car and enter the building.

Inside, the building is not too much different from the outside compared to what is usually descriptive of a general police station. There are no individuals in handcuffs, there are no officers walking from desk to desk, and there is no phone ringing off the hook with citizen complaints. Instead, all I see in this entrance corridor is a number of bilingual safety signs and a single small window dividing the general public from the receptionist. At this time, she is talking to a middle-aged man who is in need of a safety light for his child's bicycle. The receptionist immediately calls an officer who politely comes to the window, greets the father, and then gives the man a light as part of the free bicycle safety light drive the police station is conducting. She turns her attention to me, I state my name, and she opens a door to allow me to enter the main police area.

Once on the "police" side of the wall, I still wait to discover those indicators of a typical police station. An officer and I walk down a hallway, pass a kitchen and conference room, both of which are unoccupied, and enter a room toward the end of the hall. Here, two more officers wait for me. They received my letter and are here to answer my questions regarding immigration enforcement in a town that, for half of the year, is predominantly inhabited by undocumented workers. I sit down and immediately ask where everyone is. I am told that some of the officers are on patrol, and others will come for the night shift. Of course, I follow my initial question by asking, "Where are all the 'criminals'?" The answer I receive is quite surprising, for I am told that despite the concentration of undocumented immigrants in the community, crime has gone down so much in the past few years in Immokalee that the town now operates with only one jail. Traditional street crime is not an overbearing problem, which is not surprising given that research shows undocumented immigrants are less likely to participate in criminal activity due to the risk of deportation (See Martínez and Valenzuela 2006).

As my first initial visit to the Immokalee substation indicates, the issues in Immokalee are not issues of criminality. Officers do not view members of the community in terms of legal status. Rather, the officers at the Immokalee substation view everyone who lives and works in Immokalee as a member of the community. Victims will be treated as victims, and criminals will be treated as criminals, whether or not they are here legally or illegally. However, there exists the underlying issue of human trafficking and modern-day slavery, and it is this issue that legal actors must identify in order to punish offenders in the legal arena. The purpose of this chapter is to identify the efforts that are being made by legal actors in identifying and protecting victims of human trafficking, while at the same time legally punishing the offenders. This chapter will examine the three main legal agencies that are at the forefront in the legal battle against human trafficking in Immokalee: the officers of District 8, the Collier County Division of Human Trafficking, and the district attorney. However, before those groups can be considered, there must first be a discussion of immigration law and the overwhelming problems officers must overcome in order to protect victims of human trafficking despite their undocumented status. Therefore this chapter will be divided into two main sections. I will begin by discussing the traditional role of immigration enforcement at the local level, and the problems with this new role for local police. Within this same section, I will address federal statute 287(g), which allows for local police to enforce immigration law and initiate deportation. This section, although lengthy, outlines the national pros and cons associated with local-level immigration enforcement. Specifically, Collier County is a member of the 287(g) program, and therefore has the fundamental responsibility to enforce immigration laws. Consequently, there exists an inherent dilemma for officers of Immokalee, considering the underlying view of many officers that everyone is a member of the community and immigration status will not be criminalized unless there is a corresponding criminal act beyond documentation. After an overview of the national issues of immigration enforcement at the local level, I will turn the discussion to the specific legal actors associated with human trafficking in Immokalee and the proactive measures being taken to identify and protect victims of trafficking while prosecuting those responsible for the enslavement of laborers in the United States.

Understanding Local Immigration Enforcement

Research regarding the relationship between law enforcement and victims of human trafficking is divided in to two main themes: undocumented victims' unwillingness to report crime, and how law enforcement deals with enforcing immigration law at the local level. Living and working under the radar, the undocumented immigrants that are most vulnerable to victimization, nationally and in Immokalee, have been classified as a "shadow population." To understand the situation of local law enforcement in Immokalee, we must fist consider the place of this "shadow population" in the United States generally, and then the ways national issues shape enforcement at the local level.

Shadow Population

Because of their invisible status, Supreme Court Justice Brennan recognized the vulnerability of illegal and migrant populations twenty-eight years ago when he identified this population evident in the United States as a "shadow population" (*Plyler v. Doe* 1982). The shadow status in the United States is directly related to an elevated victimization rate across various types of crimes. For example, the Southern Poverty Law Center reports that between 2004 and 2007 there was a 40 percent increase in hate crimes against Latino immigrants (2009). This number continues to rise in the midst of anti-immigrant sentiments. Similarly, Wheeler et al. (2010) found that nonfatal victimizations of immigrants were comparable to those in the adult U.S.-born population (3.8 percent and 4.1 percent respectively). Beyond criminal victimizations, the smuggled and trafficked population of undocumented immigrants is vulnerable to immeasurable exploitation and neglect. Specifically, undocumented immigrants are targeted with "scams fraudulently promising status adjustment or legalization assistance" (Kittrie 2006:

1451). As discussed in earlier chapters, beyond the extreme exploitation and abuse associated with their slavery, undocumented workers residing in Immokalee are publicly victimized in a variety of ways, including scams, robbery, and assault.

Due to their vulnerable status, undocumented immigrants in Immokalee and nationwide continue to be open to criminal abuse due to a number of issues, one of which is the fear that judicial protection will result in deportation. As Kittrie noted, "'unauthorized aliens' are almost the perfect victims....They cannot turn to authorities because they have problems with their legal status....They're prime for the picking'" (quoted in Kittrie 2006: 1454). Therefore, a reciprocal relationship of distrust and criminal victimization results in the continuous abuse against undocumented immigrants.

Officers in Immokalee have reported that the fear of deportation is the leading factor for not reporting victimization. However, research has shown that other factors beyond this fear affect the underreporting of criminal victimizations in immigrant communities. In their national survey, Davis and Erez (1998) found that "immigrants [face] greater hardships when reporting crimes...including language barriers, cultural differences, and ignorance of the U.S. justice system" (2). Local police are well aware of the cultural differences that affect the underreporting of criminal victimization in immigrant communities. Davis, Erez, and Avitabile (2001) found that officers believed that "recent immigrants reported crimes less frequently than other victims" (187), which created a problem in curtailing crime in local communities. When asked about the main reasons for underreporting, the local authorities reiterated the problems of language and cultural differences.

Perhaps the greatest cultural obstacle for immigrants (documented and undocumented) is that many have a cultural "distrust of authority...without an understanding about the role of police in a democratic society" (Davis and Henderson 2003: 565). This distrust stems from illegitimate policing strategies prevalent in many second- and third-world countries. For example,

> police in many underdeveloped countries are ineffective against crime because they are poorly paid and suffer from low morale and a lack of professionalism. In fact, it is not uncommon for police to supplement their income by looking the other way when crimes are committed or by participating in criminal activity themselves (ibid.: 566).

Whether because of language barriers, cultural differences, or fear of deportation, undocumented immigrants underreport their criminal victimizations at a vast rate, both nationwide and in Immokalee. This has led to greater victimization of undocumented immigrants, as well as the ability for employers and traffickers to oppress, exploit, and neglect migrant workers throughout the country.

Enforcing Immigration Law

Although there is an inherent victimization status associated with the shadow population in the United States, as well as in Immokalee, law officers across the country now have a new role: local immigration enforcer. This has caused a greater divide in trust between immigrant communities and local police, as well as received a great amount of attention in the recent literature.

After September 11, 2001, the discussion regarding the efforts at cooperation between the local and federal authorities began to include strong criticism. The role of immigration enforcement among local police needed to be reevaluated in order to maintain national security. Part of this reevaluation included the level of immigration authority local police were able enforce.

> States and localities bear the primary responsibility for defining and prosecuting crimes. But beyond enforcing the laws or ordinances of their state or locality, state and local officials may also have the authority to enforce some federal laws, especially criminal laws. Immigration provides for both *criminal* punishments… and *civil* violations….States and localities have traditionally only been permitted to directly enforce certain *criminal* provisions that fall under their jurisdictions, whereas the enforcement of the *civil* provisions has been viewed as a federal responsibility with states playing an incidental supporting role (Seghetti et al. 2009: 1; italics in original).

After September 11, however, many states have been entering into agreements (MOAs) with the federal government to enforce both criminal and civil violations. Other states have amended their own state laws so that they may enforce criminal and civil violations without the support of the federal government. Collier County, Florida, has entered into a MOA (Memorandum of Agreement) with the federal government that now allows for trained local law enforcement in Immokalee to enforce immigration law and initiate the deportation process. Because of the new-found immigration responsibilities both in Immokalee and nationwide, immigration enforcement by local officials has received praise and criticism across the literature.

Supporters of local authorities enforcing immigration law argue that with an estimated eight to ten million undocumented immigrants living in the United States, "federal agents will never be able to do the job alone" (Sessions and Hayden 2005: 327). Because local officials are the first to encounter undocumented immigrants, they should have the ability to act in certain ways that would arguably affect the treatment of undocumented immigrants. In other words, to more effectively combat illegal immigration, local authorities should have the authority to treat civil violations (e.g., lack of legal status) in the same manner as they treat criminal violations, thereby relieving federal agents from the overwhelming task of illegal identification throughout the country.

On the other hand, critics (e.g., Arnold 2007; Miller 2002; and Olivas 2007) maintain that local immigration enforcement could have negative consequences. The first of these criticisms is that "state and local law enforcement entities will be handed an unfunded mandate and will be forced to enforce immigration law violations against their will and their expense" (Sessions and Hayden 2005: 338). Secondly, the cooperation and trust needed in order to identify victims of trafficking through victim reporting will deteriorate if victims realize the extent of immigration enforcement authorized to local authorities. Critics also maintain that local authorities will abuse their authority and engage in illegitimate practices such as racial profiling. Lastly, and perhaps most importantly, "[W]omen and children [and men] brought into the United States for the sex trade or to work in agricultural or domestic settings [should be treated] as victims of trafficking rather than immigration violators" (Miller 2002: 967). In the midst of praise and criticism, the local police in Immokalee have the obligatory duty to enforce immigration law, yet maintain a sense of community as they take proactive measures toward victim protection. The following pages will examine the unique roles and duties of the legal agents in their efforts to identify and protect victims of human trafficking while at the same time prosecuting the traffickers to the fullest extent of the law.

Law Enforcement in Immokalee, Florida

Driving through town in a police cruiser in many immigrant communities may cause an almost immediate negative reaction from the citizens. In an area so populated with undocumented migrants, one would expect to see people hide or run from the police cruiser. Building a conclusion based on my own preconceived notions regarding law enforcement and undocumented immigrants, I was amazed to see the exact opposite of my expectations. Rather than trying to hide or look away, people smiled or waved to us. When we stopped the car, members of the community would walk to the car and openly talk to us regarding their work plans and living situations. The reason for this identifiable contradiction between law enforcement and undocumented immigrants is that the police have developed a relationship of trust based on the assumption that as long as the workers do not partake in any violent or felonious criminal activities, they are welcome in the Immokalee community.

The three main legal groups working with victims of slavery are the local Immokalee law enforcement, Collier County's Division of Human Trafficking, and the district attorney. Interestingly, the contact with human trafficking victims differs by each division. For example, local law enforcement in Immokalee is more likely to have contact with the farmworkers, and their contact is most typically in response to a criminal violation. On the other hand, the Division of Human Trafficking and the district attorney work with victims of trafficking, with equal contact between victims of forced commercial sex labor and migrant farmworkers. Despite the different forms of contact, it is clear that each of these actors makes distinct attempts to reduce slavery in its various forms, from the identification of potential victims through the prosecution of the slaver. Unfortunately, there are political pitfalls to assisting undocumented immigrants, and, more and more, the legal advocates feel the pressure from the "higher-ups." Perhaps the greatest struggle between ideology and policy is that Collier County has been a participant of the national 287(g) program since 2002. To understand this conflicting status, we must first understand what the 287(g) program entails and the problems associated with it.

What Is 287(g)?

In the months following September 11, 2001, the United States Congress stressed the importance of policing the borders and reducing the number of undocumented immigrants that threaten the national security of the country. The core of this initiative was aimed at training local law enforcement to identify, detain, and begin the deportation process of undocumented immigrants within their locality. Although civil immigration enforcement became defined in 1996, local-level immigration criminalization did not become fully enforced until the creation of the Department of Homeland Security in 2002. Today the program, known as the 287(g) program of U.S. Immigration and Customs Enforcement (ICE), has become a widely sought police training program in the United States. Officers who have been trained in the program have successfully identified and charged a large number of immigrants who pose a national threat, as well as initiating the deportation hearings for hundreds of thousands of undocumented immigrants, many with violent felony convictions. The 287(g) program has arguably been successful, but in spite of this success, there exist immigrant populations in the United States that have become victim to the 287(g) program. Many are profiled and marginalized in their community, while others are victims of crime who fear deportation if they report their victimization to the police. Witnesses to crimes also fear the possibility of deportation, so many crimes go unreported.

According to the U.S. Department of Homeland Security, "the §287(g) program...allows a state and local law enforcement entity to enter into a partnership with ICE under a joint Memorandum of Agreement (MOA), in order to receive delegated authority for immigration enforcement within their jurisdiction" (www.ice.gov, accessed October 2009). In other words, law enforcement officers are deputized to act as immigration officers in their day-to-day activities. As a result, the deputizing of local law enforcement allows for the "necessary resources and latitude to pursue investigations relating to violent crimes, human smuggling, gang/organized crime activity, sexual related offenses, narcotics smuggling, and money laundering" (ibid.). As explained by Vaughan and Edwards (2009),

> The 287(g) program provides full-fledged immigration officer training to a set of local or state law enforcement officers. While state and local officers have inherent legal authority to make immigration arrests, 287(g) provides additional enforcement authority to the selected officers such as the ability to charge illegal aliens with immigration violations, beginning the process of removal... [T]he legislation was intended to give local law enforcement agencies a tool to help compensate for the federal immigration agency's limitations (p. 3).

The key limitation for which the 287(g) is meant to compensate is the limited number of ICE personnel tackling immigration enforcement nationwide. The program aims to enable those who are closest to the illegal immigration problem to become the immediate enforcers of immigration law and begin the deportation process. Notwithstanding the intentions of the program, there remain three themes of concern: the role of local law officials in enforcing immigration law, police abuse of power, and the chilling effect.

Local Officials Enforcing Immigration Law

Proponents of local police participation in immigration enforcement argue that "immigration enforcement, and in particular the 287(g) program, could serve as a criminal enforcement tool....[W]hen sophisticated criminals successfully evade criminal prosecution, an agency could use immigration enforcement as a tool to rid that community of the individual if he or she is unauthorized to be present in the United States" (Khashu 2009: 22). Supporters of the program argue that access to the federal immigration database could help identify felons who are using false identities. More importantly, law enforcement and the media have advanced the opinion that "like criminal law violators, those individuals who have violated federal immigration law are lawbreakers...[P]olice are bound to enforce federal immigration laws just as they are violations of criminal law and cannot pick and choose which laws to enforce" (ibid.: 23).

Some of the most fervent critics of the 287(g) program are the local law officials themselves. Currently, local police use certain tactics to remain in close and trusted contact with local residents. One of the key tactics used to engage immigrants is community policing. "Community policing is an approach to policing where police officers engage communities in a working partnership to reduce crime and promote public safety. It thus requires police to interact with neighborhood residents in a manner that will build trust and improve the level of cooperation with the police department" (ibid.: 24). If members of the community fear the deportation of family members or themselves, the whole philosophy of community policy is null and is only relevant to a specific set of citizens in the population. In Immokalee, this concern is not as relevant, for only a handful of officers are 287(g) certified, and according to local police officers, the dual responsibility has not disrupted their day to day local law responsibilities. Therefore, the issue of dual responsibility of law and immigration enforcement that has been acknowledged as problematic by critics of the program is not as troublesome in Immokalee as it is in other communities throughout the United States.

Another concern local law officials have acknowledged is the ever-changing nature of immigration law, and whether or not it is feasible to expect local law officials to maintain a current understanding of the law. Meissner and Kerwin (2009) found that "local police forces lack expertise in immigration law...They do not want to enforce areas of law beyond their jurisdiction, competence, and resources" (49). What Meissner and Kerwin concluded was that most police do recognize the importance of apprehending dangerous criminals as well as cooperating with ICE in "responding to crimes (such as human trafficking) which have a nexus with illegal immigration..." (ibid.: 49). However, because of the evolving immigration law, a large percentage of local police believe that general immigration enforcement should be kept as a central federal operation.

In accordance to the changing nature of immigration law is the position that those enforcing immigration policy at the local level lack any sort of federal guidance. Decker et al. (2009) found that "as local police face a new responsibility in enforcing immigration laws, they find themselves without much guidance" (273). Furthermore, "local police are often operating in something of a public policy vacuum regarding immigration law enforcement" (ibid.: 273). Decker and colleagues regard this lack of regulation and guidance as a "diffusion of governmental responsibility to more local levels and away from traditional centers of power" (ibid.: 263). With this, Decker and colleagues concluded that the decentralized system of responsibility and lack of regulation has led to various forms of police abuse of power.

Police Abuse of Power

In those states enforcing immigration law, there are two main concerns associated with police abuse of power: police raids in immigration communities and racial profiling. The concern regarding raids has developed out the now infamous 1997 Chandler Roundup at the Mexican border. Local Chandler police teamed up with federal border patrol agents to stop vehicles and question individuals who may have entered the country illegally.

> The Chandler Roundup involved officers stopping both drivers in their vehicles and individuals coming and going from the grocery stores, gas stations, and convenience stores. The Chandler Police Department checked in and around schools, stopped children, entered homes, and targeted particular businesses, all to inquire into citizenship. Many people [stated] that the police were stopping anyone who was dark-complexioned or 'Mexican-looking' and that 'non-Mexican looking' people were permitted to pass freely (Arnold 2009: 121).

The Chandler Roundup "lasted five days and resulted in the arrest and deportation of 432 undocumented immigrants, all of whom were Hispanic" (ibid 120).

Although the Chandler Roundup was not a 287(g) operation, the raid itself begs the question as to what happens when local police are given federal immigration duties. According to Vaughan and Edwards (2009), "no 287(g) agencies have engaged in street sweeps or round-ups for the sole purpose of questioning members of the community about their immigration status. All 287(g) operations and activities have been conducted in the context of criminal investigations or arrests, and for legitimate law enforcement purposes" (p. 18). However, there is evidence to support the premise that members of police trained under the 287(g) program have assisted in workplace raids. For example, Capps (2009) discusses in his research workplace raids that have occurred in Arkansas counties participating in the 287(g) program. According to Capps, "The 287(g) Task Force [in Arkansas] has concentrated heavily on identity theft and document fraud, much as ICE has across the country in recent large-scale worksite raids...The Task Force has focused on small-scale investigations and, in the largest raid to date, arrested owners and about two dozen employees of a Mexican restaurant chain in the area" (163). On the premise of fraud, police officers trained as immigration enforcers have raided restaurants, convenience stores, and homes thought to be harboring or employing undocumented immigrants.

Similarly, scholars and practitioners have expressed concern about local police using race as an indicator to make an arrest. Known as racial profiling, this practice has been regarded as an illegal tool in police enforcement. Proponents of the 287(g) program have argued that "to date, there have been no substantiated cases of racial profiling or abuse of immigration authority in any 287(g) location" (Vaughan and Edwards, 2009: 18). However, Parra-Chico (2008) has argued that officers know enough about the law to create a "prefabricated profile" to present to the courts for making a traffic stop, and "after stopping an individual, it is easy for an immigration officer to strengthen his case for reasonable suspicion through interrogation and then communicate the necessary articulable facts after the fact" (333).

Researchers (Arnold 2007; Khashu 2009; Skogan 2009, among others) have revealed that a significant number of undocumented immigrants are being targeted and stopped by 287(g) officers because of their appearance and/or color of skin. For example, Weissman and her colleagues (2009) found that

> during the month of May 2008, eighty-three percent of the immigrants arrested by Gaston County [North Carolina] ICE-authorized officers pursuant to the 287(g) program were charged with traffic violations...The arrest data appears to indicate that Mecklenburg and Alamance Counties [North Carolina] are typical in the targeting of

Hispanics for traffic offenses for the purposes of a deportation policy (29).

Weissman and her colleagues argue that local police are using their immigration authority to arrest for traffic offenses and misdemeanors rather than threats to national security. With this, they concluded that the "287(g) encourages, or at the very least tolerates, racial profiling and baseless stereotyping..." (ibid.: 29). As you will read later in this chapter, the officers of the Immokalee police department are currently feeling the bureaucratic pressure to ask for identification in all types of arrest, including traffic violations and minor misdemeanors, but refuse to check the fields or do random searches. Some advocacy-based groups have told the workers to fear the police because of raids and random identification checks, but the officers I spoke with were clear that they had no interest in conducting such activities.

The effects of racial profiling and police raids have led to the final theme of concern, which is the chilling effect.

The Chilling Effect

The chilling effect is the belief that "if local agencies become involved with immigration enforcement, immigrants in their jurisdiction will become so intimidated and fearful of local authorities that they will refrain from reporting crimes or assisting with investigations, leaving these crimes unsolved, and the perpetrators unpunished" (Vaughan and Edwards 2009: 18).

Vaughan and Edwards argue that "when immigrants do not report crimes...it is because of language and cultural factors..." (ibid.: 19). Yet, researchers and advocates vehemently express the chilling effect as a main concern regarding the 287(g) program.

The concern of a chilling effect is directly related to community policing (discussed earlier). According to Pham (2008),

> In many communities, enforcing immigration laws has complicated the relationship between local police departments and their residents. Local police, particularly within the last twenty years, have increasingly employed community policing, problem-oriented policing, and other approaches that rely on community cooperation to reduce crime. For local police working in jurisdictions with sizeable immigrant communities, enforcing immigration laws (or even being identified with that enforcement) risks cutting off that community cooperation. The concern, expressed by both police officers and immigrant advocacy groups, is that immigrants will not report crimes

or assist with criminal investigations, because they do not want to risk deportation, for themselves or undocumented family members (1308–1309).

Similarly, Khashu (2009) found that "immigrant witnesses and victims of crime, many of whom already bring with them fear and mistrust of police due to experiences with authorities in their home countries, [are not] likely to report crimes and cooperate as witnesses" (23). Immigrants have been identified as a "population particularly vulnerable to crime and particularly important as a resource in crime prevention and prosecution" (Weissman et al. 2009: 34). Because of the lack of reporting, police are not able to adequately fulfill their obligatory duty to the community. The end result is "the increasing isolation and victimization of an already vulnerable segment of society" (ibid.: 35). In Immokalee, the chilling effect has been identified as a main concern when the local police try to work with the migrant community. Because of the concerns associated with the 287(g) program, specifically the chilling effect, the members of the Collier County Sheriff's Office, specifically the Immokalee district, must negotiate their obligations of 287(g) certified immigration enforcement while maintaining a sense of trust and community in an area predominantly occupied by undocumented immigrants.

The Collier County Sheriff's Office, District 8, Immokalee

District 8 of the Collier County Sheriff's Office is a central law enforcement body that actively pursues activities to protect the citizens in the community from victimization. Located off the main street in Immokalee, District 8 has forty-five uniformed deputies serving at the station, plus six plainclothes investigators and an undetermined number of undercover narcotics officers. When I first met with officers in 2008, I found that they were very open to talk about their overall acceptance of undocumented immigrants in their community. As one officer stated, "I know it's not the sheriff's position, but it's my personal position that if they are here, and they're law abiding, I'm happy to have them. They make good neighbors. That political stuff is for someone else to fight." When asked about the criminality of the migrant workers, officers reported that they found the majority of the workers to be law abiding citizens.[1] According to one officer, "I think it would be accurate in saying that the migrant workers, like the American workers, generally are law abiding family people...But they have their percentage of criminals just as we do." Only those who have committed a felony face a real threat of deportation; as I was told, "if you are arrested for a felony, and we find out through an interview that you are here illegally, we deport you." As discussed earlier, felonious and violent activities face a real threat for deportation, for "in our program, we don't check the fields, we don't check the farms, [and] we don't check the houses." This legal attitude toward migrant workers has transpired nationally, for the way the activities associated with the 287(g) program in Immokalee are being mimicked in other 287(g) certified communities. "Over the last year, we've had a model program that's being copied in several areas of the United States, and we've spoken before Congress on our program, the ICE cooperative effort." In other words, despite the criticisms regarding profiling and marginalization associated with 287(g), the officers in Immokalee had at this time limited their immigration authority to dangerous felons, which has proven to be successful in community maintenance and crime control.

When I returned to Immokalee the following harvest season, a different story was being told. As one officer explained to me, the "higher-ups" were putting pressure on District 8 to follow through with their duties of immigration enforcement. Previously, I had been told that if an individual was arrested for a felonious activity and had a criminal history of similar crimes, or had a misdemeanor plus violence, the deportation process was to begin if the arrestee was in the United States illegally. Currently, however, any individual arrested for any crime will immediately be asked where he or she was born. If the individual is residing in Immokalee illegally, the deportation process is initiated regardless of the crime that actually took place. Therefore, more and more individuals face the threat of deportation for activities that are practically unavoidable due to the nature of illegal immigration (e.g., no valid driver's license). Unfortunately, this legal responsibility is bureaucratically forced and conflicts with the attitudes of the majority of the local officers regarding the illegal status of the migrants in the community.

One local officer I spoke with informed me that immigration enforcement was increasing not just on the streets, but also in the identification of jail inmates. I was told that between the years 2007 and 2009, of the inmates who had been questioned for residency status, approximately 70 percent were found to be present in the United States illegally. Out of approximately two thousand detained undocumented immigrants, approximately 80 percent had been removed from the United States. As indicated earlier, many of the officers in Immokalee often use their discretion when reporting the residency status of an immigrant, specifically focusing on felonious activity. This officer continued, stating that this seemed to be the attitude across Collier County. However, arrest records in Collier County indicate that approximately 75 percent of the activities for which undocumented immigrants were detained were misdemeanor violations, all of which would be eligible for deportation.

Despite the political pressure from the higher ups, the officers' attitudes toward the undocumented immigrants in the community have not changed all that much from when I first met them. After completing confidential questionnaires, I found that the overall attitude of the officers with regards to the farmworkers was positive. The majority viewed the farmworkers as members of the community (see Table 4.1).

Table 4.1: Police Attitudes Toward Illegal Farmworkers

Officers View Farmworkers As:	Members of the Community	Transient with some ties to the community	No ties to community
Percentage of officers' perceptions	50%	33%	17%

Results from questionnaires

As one officer stated, "[They are] hardworking members of the community. They shop at stores, visit restaurants, and contribute to the economy of Immokalee." Another officer stated, "I believe that they are the primary members of the community. They may be a migrant community, but during season they make up a majority of the population." However, not all responses were as community oriented. "[I view the tomato field workers as] temporary labor, [with] no ties to the community. [They are] generally law abiding (other than being illegal aliens) desperate for work." Overall, there was a trend of acceptance, but some divergence as to whether the migrant workers were part of the Immokalee community or "temporary seasonal residents" with no ties whatsoever.

Although there was a positive attitude among the officers regarding the farmworkers living in the community, those interviewed still recognized their role as law enforcement (see Table 4.2).

Table 4.2: Police Contact with Fieldworkers

Typical Police Contact	Community Policing	Victim Assistance	Crime Enforcement	Casual Citizen Encounters
Percentage of Contact Types	17%	17%	33%	33%

Results from questionnaires

When asked about their contact with the workers, the majority responded that their contact was more likely to be professional than casual. One officer reported that there was "daily contact." This officer further stated "they consume 90–95% of our law enforcement resources, i.e., responses to calls, 911 hang-ups, most all alcoholic related incidents, fights and rapes." In conjunction with the routine law enforcement response, one response listed the criminal activities associated with the migrant workers, including "drunkenness, driving without a license, crashes, fights, robberies (victims and subjects), trespassing, open container alcohol, sexual crimes, petty [sic] thefts, 90 percent of all calls possible." Another officer stated that the only contact was "routine law enforcement contact...." Although there was evidence that the officers recognized the criminal element associated with the migrant population, overall the general consensus was not one of immigration status, but one of victims and/or suspects.

> They rely on us for protection and their safe passage. We protect those who are in our community. We arrest those violating our laws. Those that are here for a couple of years or longer know that we will protect them but also know that we will deport them if they commit a crime; live here crime free and your [sic] welcome here.

As much as the officers have attempted to create a community with the farmworkers, the 287(g) is always hanging over their heads. One officer expressed concern of the current status of the 287(g) by stating:

> During the initial roll out of the 287(g) program, there was a short period of mistrust and fear of mass deportation. Effective communication by sheriff's office and practice of deporting only the worse or serious criminal illegal aliens was acceptable to the locals (legal or illegal). As we moved to target misdemeanors and smaller offenses by illegal aliens, we are experience raising levels of mistrust.

On the other hand, another comment explained that "from observing the 287(g) policy in Collier County, I believe that it's a highly effective program for taking action against the criminal elements that have illegally immigrated to the United States." This officer did not explain any further if this criminal element included misdemeanor offenses.

Whether or not the program is viewed as successful, an interesting phenomenon has emerged: there is now evidence of the chilling effect beyond the scope of the migrant workers. With the growing pressures associated with the 287(g), a chilling effect appears to be growing among officers when faced with the decision to arrest an immigrant whose status is questionable. For example, it was acknowledged in the Immokalee substation that if an officer pulls over a farmworker who has returned to the community year after year, the officer may just give a verbal warning if the farmworker is guilty of no more than a simple driving violation. Although the crimes for which farmworkers are being arrested are similar season after season (driving without a license, open container, fights, petty thefts, etc.), arrest records reveal an initial decrease followed by a subsequent increase throughout the harvest seasons (see Table 4.3).

Table 4.3: Percent of Arrestees Born Outside the United States

Year	Nov.	Dec.	Jan.	Feb.	Mar.	Apr.
2008	30%	39%				
2009	23%	33%	30%	35%	39%	27%
2010			30%	52%	50%	51%

Collier County Arrest Log (www.colliersheriff.org)

As Table 4.3 indicates, there was a general decrease in arrests between the two harvest seasons, followed by an increase in the later months. When I asked the officers why this change in arrest numbers is occurring, I was given no response, and therefore I independently analyzed a number of issues that may explain the switch from a decrease in arrests to an increase in arrests. The first is that trust may have been building between law enforcement and the migrant workers, allowing for more of the workers to move into the community. With an influx of workers, there may also have been an increase in criminal violations. A larger social reason for the increase is that the officers may have felt more pressure due to the new national focus on immigration. In January 2010, Arizona Senator Russell Pearce introduced the controversial Senate Bill 1070. With the introduction of this bill, national attention was drawn to the porous U.S. borders, as many supported a tougher stance against undocumented immigrants in the United States. The reemergence of the focus on illegal immigration may have forced the hand of the 287(g) officers to more fully enforce their immigration duties causing an increase in arrests of migrant farmworkers residing in the United States illegally.

Regardless of the cause for the change in arrest patterns, the violations for which the farmworkers were being arrested remained the same. Driving violations (no valid driver's license, suspended or expired license, failure to register vehicle, and DUI) were the majority of the arrests associated with those arrested with another country of origin. From the months of November through April, driving violations averaged 52 percent of the arrests, with the high being 86 percent of the overall immigrant arrests in March 2010 and the low being 42 percent of the overall immigrant arrests in April 2010. The second most common offense associated with the immigrants in Immokalee is "open container." Over the six months and two harvest seasons, arrests for open container were an average of 24 percent of all immigrant arrests. The third most common offense was assault/battery, many of which were deemed domestic violence cases. These violations averaged to be 18 percent of the overall immigrant arrests over the two seasons I investigated.

It should be reiterated that the types of offenses for which immigrants are being arrested have remained the same, but those offenses that initiate the deportation process are changing. Over the duration of two years, there has been a shift from the deportation of dangerous felons who threaten the safety of the community toward the more frequent deportation of illegal migrant workers who have been arrested for any offense, including minor misdemeanors.[2] This has led to a constant negotiation of officers' duties combined with their community duties. This system of negotiation has led the officers to develop new strategies to build a system of trust and safety in a community of undocumented immigrants.

Proactive Measures Made by Local Police

Immokalee officers do realize the extent of victimization in the fields and have therefore incorporated a number of proactive strategies to help reduce the victimization of farm workers. One of these programs is known as "coffee with the migrant."

> The picking season generally or the migrant season for Immokalee is during the winter months. So, of course, in the morning hours, kind of brisk and cool, a nice cup of coffee is inviting. We'll get private donors to just donate coffee. We've bought some huge pots of coffee, and we'll just open the tailgate or a collapsible table and say 'C'mon guys, free coffee!' And as they come up for free coffee…it is sort of like watching penguins jump into the water. Whose gonna be first? You or me? And one finally comes up and gets a free cup of coffee and sees nothing happens to them, everybody comes.

The purpose of "coffee with the migrant" is not just to give away free coffee, but also to incorporate a relationship of trust between the officers and the workers, as well as present preventative safety measures that the workers may utilize in their everyday lives. When the migrant approaches the coffee stand, he is given safety information:

> "Hey, by the way, did you know that bar right there that you guys all drink at? We got a bunch of bad guys hanging out waiting for you to leave stupid drunk. So when you walk home, walk in twos and threes. Or have a designated walker."

Every season, the local police also choose a problem associated with victimization to be a principal mission. The first season I met with the local police, protecting the migrants from being a victim of the guato-lotto was their mission. Officers discussed a number of activities to reduce the economic victimization of the migrant workers. The first of these was to introduce personal alarms for the workers to carry. If they were robbed, they could pull a cord and an alarm would be set off that would draw community attention to the crime as it occurs. Unfortunately, there has not been enough money or support to fund a device for every worker. Another activity is initiating a way in which the workers could safely deposit their cash instead of carrying it around with them. The biggest problem with safeguarding the cash has been the lack of proper identification and fear of outing a worker's legal status. However, the current situation is extremely dangerous for the worker. For example, there was a case of a migrant worker who was stopped by the police. The police found $18,000 in cash that he was carrying. He had been carrying it for so long that there was mold growing on the bills. Although this was an extreme case, many of the workers carry large sums of cash, which creates a system of easy targeting for the criminals.

During the following season, the local police had embarked on an initiative to identify and protect the women and girls forced into commercial sexual exploitation. This mission was especially interesting because the police usually focused their attention on the general criminality (e.g. public drunkenness and no valid driver's license) and the identified economic victimization (i.e. guatto-lotto) of the farmworkers, whereas they would assist the women as victims if the women were identified as such. However, with an increase of media attention on forced commercial sexual labor that highlighted the vulnerabilities of many young women in immigrant communities, it was impossible for the police to turn their back on the prostitution evident in Immokalee. Because their relationship with the women in the brothels was on a different level than their relationship with the field workers, the police felt it necessary to utilize the local nonprofit groups to assist in the processes of identification and protection. As a proactive strategy, the police were to support sexual education initiatives as well as provide free sexual protection for the women working in the brothels.

A previous mission initiated the demands of better living conditions for the field workers. Landlords were confronted to reduce the rates of rent, as well as reduce the numbers of workers living in a unit. Although many areas of Immokalee appear as they always have, with four, five, or six people living in a one-room shed, there are other areas showing signs of improvement and progression toward safer living standards. In fact, during this mission of housing improvement, FEMA donated a number of trailers for the workers to inhabit. Because this is federal housing, the trailers are maintained to meet county standards, and each has a capacity of the number of residents, generally ranging from four to six.

Overall, the officers of District 8 have made strong attempts at improving the life conditions for the workers inhabiting the community eight months of the year. Perhaps the grassroots attitude can be best summed up with the following quote: "They are in our community; Legal or illegal, they are still here. If someone gets thumped, we need to know about it so we can deal with it, and put the bad guy in jail....We don't look at those legal illegal issues when they are the victim...and we like that."

Whereas the local police have the sole mission of protecting victims of crime while punishing the criminals, there are two major agencies that focus on protecting and empowering victims of human trafficking and prosecuting offenders: the Collier County Division of Human Trafficking and the assistant US district attorney of southwest Florida.

Collier County Division of Human Trafficking

Initiated in 2004, the Collier County Division of Human Trafficking is directly involved with improving the lives of migrant workers, specifically those who have been trafficked into the United States. When I first met with the Division in 2009, there were a total of three people in the office: two sworn officers and a victim's advocate. Today, there is only one detective and the victim's advocate. These two individuals have the responsibility of enforcing the laws against human trafficking and assisting victims throughout all of Collier County.

The detective and advocate make every effort to insure the protection of victims who come forward and speak out against a slaver. Victims are taken to secure locations and have access to the victim's advocate 24/7. Victims are provided money, food, clothing, and housing while awaiting the prosecutorial process, as well as health care and other social services. After the prosecution of a trafficker, the advocate assists the victim in finding employment or education. Only when victims choose to leave the safe location or contact their traffickers is their protection compromised.

The Division also partakes in distinctive activities to assist victims in Immokalee. The first of these is referred to as the Migrant Matrix. This event usually takes place in October or November to coincide with the beginning of the harvest season. Working together with the Coalition of Immokalee Workers (CIW) (see Chapter 6), the Division contributes to producing a social event that is similar to a block party. This is evidence of a unique relationship between the Division of Human Trafficking and the CIW, for, as I was told a number of times by the members of the District 8 substation, there is a strained relationship between the two groups. As one local officer explained, "[The CIW's] goal is more of a political agenda…With their mission and focus, I think they are forgetting who they are serving—their client….At times, we are on the same page…and other times…we just don't see eye to eye." On the other hand, the members of the Division of Human Trafficking spend hours at the CIW headquarters, and are able to call each other for assistance. There is a very personal and affable relationship between the two groups.

During the Migrant Matrix, food and beverages are served as speakers take the center stage to educate the workers on the different outlets that assist in reducing victimization. During the migrant matrix, members of the Division will get on stage and explain to the workers the different indicators of trafficking, as well as provide contact information for anyone who has been trafficked into the area or someone they may know who is currently bonded to a trafficker. Although there is an initial element of mistrust of law enforcement, the migrant matrix provides an introduction for victims who need out of their trafficked bondage.

Aside from the Migrant Matrix, the members of the Division also educate migrant workers on a local one-to-one level. Particularly at the beginning of the harvest season, but also throughout the season, Division members will drive and walk around Immokalee handing out fliers (in both Spanish and English) that define human trafficking. Included in the fliers are the basic facts about trafficking and the Trafficking Victims Protection Act. More important is information for the migrant workers that will help them identify indicators of human trafficking and persons to contact if they suspect someone they know is a victim of trafficking (to see a sample of the flier that is handed to potential victims of trafficking, see Appendix B). As already stated, members of the Division may also hang out at CIW headquarters to promote visibility while becoming less of a "law enforcement threat." To illustrate the level of trust that has been developed by the members of the Division of Human Trafficking, during one visit in which I was invited to ride along on a visit to Immokalee, we had to travel in an unmarked truck. The reason was that the workers were completely comfortable to approach the detective and advocate and ask for money or other services. The detective and advocate knew of my research and how much time would be needed for us to be in Immokalee if I were to be able to gather valuable information, so they decided to avoid the hassle and travel through the town incognito.

As with the District 8 officers, the Division members struggle with a chilling effect. Migrant workers fear repercussions for talking with law enforcement. Although Division members do their best to educate the workers, as well as reiterate that they are there to help rather than deport, many of the workers fear that their families will be killed by the traffickers or that the police will deport them if their illegal status is discovered. The officer and advocate explained that they must continue to "earn trust through education."

Another interesting problem the Division members face is that the migrant workers do not see themselves as victims. For example, there was a case of a couple who sought assistance from the Division of Human Trafficking for one of the couple's family members. As the officers spoke with the couple, they quickly learned that this couple had been trafficked into Immokalee as well. However, when asked about their own victimization, the couple asserted that they did not require assistance, only their family members who they believed had been trafficked.

Because there is limited cooperation from the victims, the officers rely not only on the accounts of other workers, but also on proactive policing. This involves driving around the town of Immokalee looking for indicators of human trafficking and abuse. One indicator is poor housing conditions. As stated earlier in the book, many of the homes have several people living in a small space. The space itself may be substandard, with broken floorboards, peeling paint, fallen shutters, and overgrown lawns. Officers explained to me that many of these homes will be grouped together in small communities, and that is a strong indicator that all of the workers living there work on the same tomato field, and are most probably in debt to the same trafficker. As highlighted in Chapter 3, this type of housing is also an indication of a brothel. Locations that display the obvious brothel indicators are observed by the Division members to determine if men suddenly begin to come and go from the building throughout the day.

Although there have been many obstacles for those working in the Division of Human Trafficking, there have also been many successes. Since its origination, the Division alone has assisted in two successful federal prosecutions and two more local prosecutions. This number may be considered low, but in the context of the time the Division has been active, as well as the limited number of officials, the work that has been done regarding prosecutions is quite significant. With the aid of the Division, a number of victims have been removed from their bonded condition and granted an improved life while in the United States. Many have completed high school; some have found employment and have earned temporary visas, while many others now have access to health care, housing, and other social services. The Division of Human Trafficking has made great efforts in improving the lives of those who have been trafficked and enslaved in Immokalee, but that is only one portion of the equation. The prosecution of the offenders of trafficking lies in the hands of the assistant US district attorney of southwestern Florida.

Assistant U.S. District Attorney of Southwest Florida

In 1999, a slavery case in southwestern Florida was brought to the district attorney's office by the Department of Justice. According to the assistant US district attorney:

> [In Immokalee], three men were in a fist fight. Two men were beating up another man, and the deputies came and broke it up. One of the guys—one of the aggressors said, "You owe me $5,000." And the

deputy was bright enough to think how does one bring up a $5,000 debt in a migrant camp? And it led them to the deliberation of 22 people who were being held in two double-wides that had been smuggled in.

Through investigation, it was found that approximately thirty workers, mostly undocumented Mexican migrants, were forced to pick tomatoes for no pay. Workers were violently abused, including being run down with a car, and told they could not leave until they paid off their debt, which was between $1,500 and $5,000 per worker. Abel Cuello and co-conspirators were sentenced to a combined five years plus restitution ($29,000) to the victims (*United States v. Cuello* 1999). This case was considered the introduction to a multitude of human trafficking cases in Immokalee, including the prosecution of the Navarrete brothers outlined in the introduction of the book.

One of the most difficult dilemmas of prosecuting a slavery case is that the victim is in the United States illegally. As told to me by the assistant US district attorney:

> The thing that is unspoken in slavery prosecutions by the defense is that they are illegals. They deserve whatever they get when they come here. They know that they're illegals... So what? It's basically their word that they are lying to stay here. And so my job is basically twofold: to convince American juries that slavery exists and then convince them why they should care.

Part of doing this is explaining to the jury that no matter how an individual got into the United States, the fact of the matter is that this individual is here. Once that is so, the law must take into account that the undocumented immigrant is a human being and to make sure that the individual is not victimized by a money-making criminal enterprise. The assistant US district attorney continued to explain:

> Whenever anybody crosses the border and is in our country, we have a certain obligation to make sure that our laws are not violated, regardless of where they came from or how they came here. That's why I've always said I don't believe slavery in the United States today should be in the same sense. What I do believe is that illegal aliens are not a problem, that they are people. And so, what we try and do is first empower them. But second of all, just like any other criminal organization, whether it be drugs or guns or anything, my idea is that it is all about the money. These people are now just money makers for the slavers, and my job is to make their life unprofitable, which we are able to do by forfeitures, and taking the money that they have made—

taking their homes sometimes....The deal is you prepare like every other criminal case, but the one advantage that you have in other cases is that...juries understand that drugs are bad and that they are prevalent. They understand that child pornography is bad and that it is prevalent. And most people, in many areas, don't understand that there is a slavery problem and would not believe that it is literally in their back yard.

To prosecute a slaver case, the prosecutor is dependent on not only the local police, but also the information derived from nongovernmental organizations. The assistant US district attorney claimed that "the most unique thing about slavery prosecutions is that someone that is in a nongovernmental organization [is always included] in the part of the prosecution team." The prosecutors rely on the expertise of nongovernmental organizations such as the CIW and Zonta International, a woman's organization that has taken slavery as one of its central missions. This is a radical idea, because the NGOs become an integral part of the prosecuting team. The members of the NGOs are able to identify victims, corroborate victim stories, and advocate on the victim's behalf. Earlier in the book, I discussed an instance of a man claiming to own a young girl's soul, which was why she was his slave. The information that the young girl provided to advocates actually assisted the prosecution. The assistant US district attorney described to me the following:

> [B]ecause part of their religion—off-shoot of Santeria—[the man] had cut off a lock of her hair and he kept it with him at all times. I [the prosecutor] would have never found out about that lock of hair, but for the nongovernment organization person finding out about it. And sure enough, I went back to the booking sheet, and there, taken off of him at the time of his arrest, was a vial of hair. You can imagine how powerful that is for an American jury to see.

Members of the NGO are able to understand the mindset and culture of the victim. As a result, victims are able to communicate information to members of the NGOs that they feel may be unimportant to the prosecutor. It is this information that is then passed to the prosecution that makes for a stronger case.

Beyond the relationship with advocates, the prosecution effort is literally a team effort:

> I am only part of a team. The investigators that have been trained in human trafficking in this area are very talented—very good. And then, I do have a Department of Justice attorney who assists, because it is a

very high priority in the Department of Justice, and in…these types of cases, you know that phrase "We're from Washington, we're here to help,"…that is very true. They do help…

As the prosecutor stated, "I have very little in common with a fifteen-year old Guatemalan girl," but (with the assistance of NGOs, local detectives and police officers, plus federal assistance), "somebody on the prosecution team does."

Another unique aspect of slavery prosecution is the use of media and education.

Every time somebody reads…or hears a documentary on [slavery], they'll think of a situation where there might have been slavery and they didn't think to ask two or three more questions. When I speak, that's kind of the look of dawning comprehension that I see on law enforcement officers, that is "Oh—I remember a situation—I knew something wasn't right and I didn't know to ask these three more questions: 'Who is paying you the money?' or 'What kind of money are you getting?' or 'Do you receive any money?' or situations where the person is not allowed to speak—that somebody always speaks for them."

By relying on media coverage, positive or negative, law enforcement and ordinary citizens are more able to identify situations of slavery and bring them to the attention of the prosecutor. Most recently, after a series of newspaper articles, there were seven reports of slavery that followed; six of them turned out to be legitimate.

The identification of victims and the prosecutions of slavers are not distinctive to Immokalee, but the networking with other organizations has proven to be successful in that for every trafficking case that has been charged in Immokalee, the slavers have incurred some form of punishment. The assistant US district attorney explained to me that:

Southwestern Florida has more slavery cases than most states. We have a heightened community awareness and we have a diverse population. You can hide in plain sight here. We have all kinds of people here. So you can be a wealthy Venezuelan couple, and decide you're going to bring up somebody from Venezuela who thinks she's going to go to school. And when she gets here, she becomes a prisoner in the home. They make her a domestic servant. Because of our agricultural population, we have a large degree of migrant workers, most of whom are illegal. And then we also have sexual slavery because we have the tourism industry and we have a lot of transients. [The slavers] have a network that can move [the victims] from Orlando to Tampa so the girls never actually know where they are. So we have all three kinds. The reason again we have so many cases is not because other areas don't have the same amount of cases—it's just that we have nongovernmental organizations...[and local police] that can spot them...and so they are sensitive to what may be a slavery case.

In other words, it is not only the number of trafficking cases that has generated much attention for Immokalee. It is the networking of legal actors, and as will be illustrated in the next chapter, local advocates, that has proven to be successful in identifying victims of the forms of trafficking evident in Immokalee while successfully prosecuting the slavers.

Conclusion

Legal actors in Immokalee have the unique duty of enforcing immigration law while at the same time protecting the undocumented citizens of their community. The steps that have been take in Immokalee serve as an example for other communities that are faced with a similar dilemma with regards to immigration law and human trafficking. However, before any proactive measures may be taken, one major issue must be addressed: trafficking victim identification by legal professionals.

Since the implementation of the Trafficking of Victims Protection Act (2000), local law enforcement has had the tedious task of identifying victims of human trafficking and interpreting and implementing new laws associated with trafficking. Unfortunately, major divergences still exist with respect to training officers to identify human trafficking, as well as how to overcome biases related to illegal immigration and victim complicity.

Research has consistently shown a pattern of officers receiving little to no training in how to identify a victim of human trafficking. For example, Farrell et al. (2007) surveyed medium to large police departments nationwide and found that only 40 percent had received some sort of training. Similarly, Wilson et al. (2006) found that the majority of the responding departments in their survey "did not have specific policy, procedures, and training addressing human trafficking" (158). Because of the limited training, officers are often ill-prepared to identify and investigate cases of human trafficking. Due to this lack of preparation, victims are able to "hide in plain sight" while the officers are unable to identify these victims as such. In the most extreme cases, victims are arrested for the criminal actions inherently associated with trafficking rather than receiving the deserved protection and assistance from the local police.

As Farrell et al. noted, "[T]rafficking cases require law enforcement to re-categorize and re-prioritize behavior that has long existed as its own crime type" (2007: 21). For example, what was once considered a case of prostitution must now be examined under the definition of trafficking. Is the prostitute a criminal, or was she forced or coerced into a prostitution ring? "[E]ven when officers believe the behavior is serious, the victims are worthy of protection, and the crime necessitates special categorization, they often still have difficulty in identifying such new crimes" (ibid.: 23). Therefore, there is a constant need to "redefine old problems with new labels and enhanced priorities" (ibid.).

A third difficulty with respect to the ill-preparation of local officers to tackle human trafficking within their communities is overcoming their own prejudices toward immigrants. Some officers believe that the victims they encounter are "complicit in their own victimization" (ibid.: 20). This is especially true when the victim of trafficking is a male farm laborer or an adult female forced into sexual slavery. Due to their maturity or stereotypical role as protector, "authorities [fail] to notice the victims [as victims] and [do not] take the appropriate action to bring them to safety" (Wilson and Dalton 2008: 304). Even an officer who believes the victim to be only partially to blame for his or her victimization may be reluctant to apply the label to that individual. Until these biases are overcome, trafficked individuals will continue to be neglected and abused within the borders of the United States.

With these problems associated with victim identification, local officers across the country need to implement a training program that educates street level officers in the key indicators of human trafficking, such as someone else speaking for the victim, lack of identity, and physical trauma. Beyond the identification process, officers and prosecutors need to call human trafficking "human trafficking." In order to get an accurate picture of human trafficking in the United States, we must increase the number of human trafficking prosecutions. In many cases, there is clear evidence of trafficking, yet the prosecutor does not believe a trafficking conviction is likely. Therefore, the charges will be reduced to neglect, harboring, sexual assault, etc. Because the cases are not charged as trafficking cases, the victim will not get the benefits associated with being a victim of trafficking, such as the T-Visa.[3]

In addition to being able to identify victims of trafficking, as well as labeling incidents of trafficking correctly, law enforcement officials throughout the United States may also draw on the developed relationship between the legal actors in Immokalee and the undocumented citizens of the community. The officers in Immokalee have initiated a relationship with the undocumented immigrants so as to protect the citizens from victimization. Although this relationship is far from perfect, as witnessed by the extreme exploitation and abuse experienced by the immigrants in Immokalee illustrated in the earlier chapters, the legal officials have taken proactive measures in attempts to build a relationship between the workers and the police. Whether it is a block party, such as the Migrant Matrix, or daily coffee with the workers, in conjunction with advocates, the police have developed a unique relationship with the local community. They are able to drive through worker housing areas without causing a mass fleeing of the residents. The system of trust has been in development for a number of years and still needs much work, but the police have made it clear that, although they have the responsibility to enforce immigration law, they will not conduct mass raids or bang on doors demanding identification. Law enforcement agencies throughout the United States that have signed MOAs and work in highly populated immigration communities may learn from the Immokalee example that beyond the criminal identification associated with illegal immigration, undocumented workers have the ability to add to and help maintain a community. As I was told by local officers in Immokalee, whether immigrants are here legally or illegally, they are here, and "Our goal is… to make it safe and improve the quality of life for the migrant worker."

In relation to creating a system of trust between law enforcement and the undocumented workers, the legal actors in Immokalee have taken proactive measures to be a part of the community in that they are visible and talk with the migrants on a daily basis. This relationship is key to identifying and protecting victims of trafficking and the everyday crime associated with their shadow status. Other officers I have talked to, outside of Immokalee, confirmed that they do not maintain a visible presence in the immigrant community, for they believe it could be harmful to the victims in that the traffickers themselves many times are residents of the same community. However, the visibility of the police is beneficial in a number of ways. First of all, it puts pressure on the traffickers if indeed they are also residing in the immigrant community. Police visibility may reduce visible exploitation of the undocumented immigrants. Secondly, the presence of the police creates an outlet for victims who are willing to take the risk to be identified and escape their life of trafficking. In addition to victims reporting on themselves, police who have a relationship with members of the community are also able to filter out the criminal element as distinct from victimized immigrants. This is particularly important when labeling trafficking, for the stronger the relationship between the police and the community, the more likely they will be able to identify human trafficking and have it be prosecuted as such, rather than as a harboring, sexual assault, or robbery charge. Lastly, the trust developed through constant visibility may reduce the chilling effect, because immigrants, as they learn that the police are not there to deport those with an undocumented status, will be more likely to turn to the police and report their victimization. The principal actions taking place in Immokalee by legal actors have created a community, albeit one of "illegal immigration," with reduced levels of victim and crime assistance, and this community has been maintained through police visibility, trafficking identification and trafficking charges, as well as proactive techniques to improve the levels of trust.

Lastly, officers, detectives, and prosecutors must be willing to network with one another, as well as with nongovernmental organizations. Networking has proven to be successful in both identifying victims and prosecuting the offenders. Each legal actor I spoke with stressed the importance of networking. Human trafficking occurs in virtually every community in the United States, but it is the training and sensitivity to trafficking in the community that has brought attention to Immokalee.

Overall, the police officers at the Immokalee substation, the Division of Human Trafficking, and the office of the district attorney are in a unique position not only to reveal the existence of slavery in the United States, but also to try to get people to care about those who are enslaved. Through diligent efforts, and with the assistance of NGOs and the power of education and media, every slavery case identified in southwestern Florida that has been prosecuted has been successful. Proactive measures by the local police to assist in victim identification, as well as a concerned district attorney's office, have brought Immokalee recognition not only as a central hub of human trafficking, but also as an area where caring officials are making great strides in eradicating modern-day slavery in this small Florida community. However, the battle against human trafficking and slavery in Immokalee is not just a battle to be fought by the law enforcement and legal advocates. As already indicated, another major player in the identification and protection of victims of trafficking and slavery is the nongovernmental groups. Law officials are unable to act without the assistance of NGOs, and NGOs are unable to move beyond identification without the assistance of all levels of law enforcement.

[1] The interviews with the police specified their contact with migrant workers because preliminary research indicated that their legal duties were more often associated with the farmworkers rather than the victims of sexual slavery.

[2] There is one exception to the deportation rule. If a migrant worker who is arrested can provide evidence of being trapped in a system of slavery as well as being trafficked into the United States, the officers will treat the individual as a victim rather than a criminal.

[3] "The T Nonimmigrant Status (T visa) protects victims of human trafficking and allows victims to remain in the United States to assist in an investigation or prosecution of human trafficking" (United States Citizenship and Immigration Services, www.uscis.gov, 2011).

5

Community Responses

"When spider webs unite, they can tie up a lion."
—Ethiopian Proverb

In early summer 2008, I receive an email from the United Students Against Sweatshops (USAW) listserv. The email informs me that members of the Coalition of Immokalee Workers (CIW) will be protesting in St. Louis, Missouri, and asks for supporters of the cause to join the protest. At this point I have been researching the Coalition for a number of months, but haven't yet had a chance to meet or talk with any of the members. Not only was I an advocate for the cause, but I felt that this would be a great time to introduce myself and possibly make some contacts for future research. So I get in my car and drive half an hour to University City, Missouri, to attend a protest against Chipotle Mexican Grill.

The protesters had taken their local campaign of a Penny More per Pound on a national tour, staging activities outside the companies comprising a large percentage of the bulk tomato consumers across the United States.[1] These companies included Chipotle Mexican Grill, Taco Bell, Whole Foods, and Burger King among others. I arrive at the site of the protest expecting to see a great "hoopla" of media and local advocates joining in the protest, as well as a strong police presence protecting the property of Chipotle. However, just a handful of Immokalee workers are handing out fliers to passers-by on the street, and a single individual with a megaphone is describing the atrocities associated with the modern tomato industry. No one would stop to listen; no one seemed to care.

I try to talk with some of the workers handing out the informational fliers, but they do not speak to the passers-by, keeping their eyes focused on their own hands as they pass the information from one disinterested person to the next. A friend who is with me at the time comments that the workers seem to be completely scared and downtrodden. I explain to her that many of these individuals have endured such a horrific experience associated with the cycle of migration and slavery that perhaps many have lost their own personal hope, but they still continue to protest on behalf of those still trapped in the cycle, as well as the next generation of migrant workers. The lack of support that these workers are receiving from the general public is appalling; surely some level of verbal abuse has met the tour as it made its way across the country, for the reality is that the general public outside of Immokalee is completely unaware of the slave labor that continues to exist in our own backyard.

Although members of the Collier County Sheriff's Office and the assistant US district attorney have the difficult task of identifying victims and punishing offenders, their work will conclude in one of two ways: at the end of a trial, or with the victim refusing to assist in the prosecution. The law is not required to assist the victim whenever these ends are met. Therefore, advocate groups throughout southern Florida have the extraordinary mission of identifying and protecting victims of human trafficking before, during, and after the trial, in addition to the larger responsibility of educating various agencies and individuals on how to combat human trafficking throughout the country and the world. This chapter focuses specifically on three distinct nongovernmental organizations that participate in various levels of advocacy. Two groups, the Human Trafficking Awareness Task Force and Catholic Charities, focus their attentions more on victims of forced commercial sex labor, whereas the third group, the Coalition of Immokalee Workers, is purely devoted to improving the life conditions of migrant laborers. Even within the agencies, the organizational missions are distinct, varying from education to national protests against slavery consumerism. Therefore, this chapter spends a substantial amount of time discussing the actors and missions of three organizations that have made tremendous strides in drawing national attention to slavery in Immokalee, as well as assisting in the identification and prosecution of those responsible for the continuation of modern-day slavery. In addition, this chapter briefly highlights the neighboring community and local media reactions to slavery in Immokalee. Although this last section is brief, it provides an overall account of how community members perceive trafficking in their locality. However, before each group is discussed, it is important to present the general significance of nongovernmental organizations in the battle against human trafficking. Therefore, this chapter will begin with a brief overview of the desired characteristics and expectations of nongovernmental organizations if they are to successfully impact the elimination of human trafficking.

Desired Characteristics of Nongovernmental Organizations

The work of nongovernmental organizations (NGOs) is crucial to the safety and welfare of trafficked victims. However, in order to fulfill their obligation, a number of things are expected of the NGOs. First, the NGO must provide adequate shelter to the trafficked victims. Many times, victims are housed in prisons or detention centers while they await deportation or their time to testify at trial. According to Tiefenbrun, "[victims] should be placed in appropriate safe shelters providing medical, psychological, and social services, including translation" (2002: 156). The Trafficking of Victims Protection Act (TVPA) of 2000 states: "Victims of severe forms of trafficking, while in the custody of the Federal Government...shall not be detained in facilities inappropriate to their status as crime victims; receive necessary medical care and other assistance; and be provided protection..." (Public Law 106–386—Oct. 28, 2000 114 STAT. 1477). In other words, victims of trafficking must receive adequate shelter and necessary services so that they will not be revictimized as they begin the recovery process.

It is also expected that NGOs will assist trafficked victims in obtaining a T visa. In 2002, the attorney general approved the T visa regulation in accordance with the TVPA 2000. According to the Department of Justice,

> The T visa is specifically designed for certain human trafficking victims who cooperate with law enforcement against those responsible for their enslavement. The statute allows victims to remain in the United States if it is determined that such victims could suffer "extreme hardship involving unusual and severe harm" if returned to their home countries. After three years in T status, victims of human trafficking may apply for permanent residency. In addition, subject to some limitations, the regulation allows victims to apply for non-immigrant status for their spouses and children (U.S. Department of Justice 2002).

Eventually, it would be ideal that the T visa be extended beyond those victims who cooperate with law enforcement, mainly because the threats posed against the victims' families and the victims themselves may deter many from stepping forward against their trafficker. However, at this point in the battle against human trafficking, it is imperative that those working with NGOs educate their clients on the possibility of a T visa if the client agrees to cooperate in the prosecution of the trafficker.

Third, NGOs are expected to develop partnerships with local law enforcement, prosecutors, community leaders, and the government. According to Joshi (2002):

> Many non-profit organizations, geared to helping trafficking victims, seek to assist them in any way they can…Cooperation between federal and state governmental agencies and the nonprofit groups that trafficking victims turn to is vital to the well-being of the victims. Without such cooperation, the already limited resources of each would be further stretched to the detriment of those victims. Victims of trafficking are often dependent on agencies that seek to help them repatriate to their home countries and reintegrate into their society (35–36).

In addition, "although NGOs are driving the global anti-trafficking movement, Governments remain vital because they are the ones that establish anti-trafficking policies, strengthen law enforcement, and fund support for victims" (Yu Perkins: 2005: 55). Each agency in the anti-trafficking movement will only be as effective as the other agencies it assists. Therefore, cooperation must exist at all levels of the movement, from the NGOs to the federal government.

It is also imperative that the members of the NGO do not revictimize the client. Critics (see Mutua 2001; and Bhabha 2003) have argued that many times, human rights organizations revictimize the client by telling the story of the victim to raise awareness of the problem. As noted by Haynes, "[A]dvocates should be careful of what narratives they use when telling the stories of those abused, as by telling any victim's story they risk furthering the 'victim subject' paradigm" (2006: 1). Haynes goes on to argue that in order to empower the victim, the way she is recognized must be altered. According to Haynes, "[Advocates must] acknowledge that the client 'owns' the problem and its solution, understand the motivations involved…, and generally counsel with the understanding that the client is the primary decision-maker in the relationship" (ibid.: 17). Therefore, members of the NGO working with the victim must let her be the center, rather than the object, of the solution.

Perhaps one of the most important expectations of the NGO is for the members of the organization to raise public awareness. Many times, victims of human trafficking are brought to the attention of local law enforcement through the calls of concerned citizens. However, many citizens do not recognize the key indicators that may identify a victim of human trafficking. It is therefore imperative that the members of the NGOs educate the public on these common indicators. This involves "active outreach by speaking to different communities...about issues related to human trafficking" (Yu Perkins 2005: 55). Not only will the community be more aware of human trafficking, but "vulnerable individuals, such as the poverty stricken who seek employment abroad...[will] understand the process of trafficking...[and] avoid being victims" (ibid.: 54).

In sum, in order to assist the victims of human trafficking while reducing the demand, members of the NGOs are expected to provide the necessary services that will improve the life conditions of the trafficked client while empowering the client to move beyond the stigma of being a victim and an undocumented immigrant. Beyond this, advocates fighting against human trafficking will take innumerable measures in protecting victims while, at the same time, making every effort to punish the offenders. Consider the following story I was told first-hand: the story of Rosa, and one amazing advocate who was determined to protect and empower one individual victim of human trafficking.

The story of Rosa is an extraordinary example of one advocate's mission to expose the ugliness hidden behind the walls of seemingly ordinary families.[2] It is the story of the everyday people disposed of in order to conceal the truth. It is a story that needs to be told over and over again not only to illustrate the atrocities of human trafficking, but also to shine a light on the measures that are taken to protect one victim and punish the offender.

Rosa was twelve years old when she was transferred to a foster home so that she could be closer to her sister, Ana. Ana had been identified as a victim of human trafficking at the age of thirteen. At this time, she and her infant child were living in a foster home with a local advocate, Andrea. Ana explained to Andrea that her younger sister had been moving from foster home to foster home, and after an initial interview, Andrea recognized in Rosa, just as she had with Ana, all the indicators of a trafficking victim. Unfortunately, Andrea could not take in any more foster children, but she was able to place Rosa with a family only a few blocks away. For the next four years, Rosa spent countless hours at Andrea's home, but when Ana aged out of foster care, Rosa suddenly stopped visiting.

Andrea was able to maintain contact with Ana, so it was not a surprise when Ana called her one afternoon seeking assistance in finding her sister. Rosa had been missing for a number of weeks, and Ana had no way of finding her. After a time of independent investigation, Andrea uncovered an almost unimaginable nightmare that Rosa had been enduring for four years. From the beginning of her placement in the new foster home four years earlier, Rosa's foster father had raped her almost every night.

Andrea assisted Rosa in filing charges against the foster father. Rosa's foster mother, however, had no intention of seeing her husband go to prison because of a young girl's "seduction," and so, she confiscated Rosa's United States passport, provided her with an illegal falsified passport, and put her on the next plane to Guatemala. With no documentation, Rosa would not be able to legally reenter the United States.

When Andrea heard what had happened to Rosa, she implored the prosecutor to assist her in bringing Rosa back to the United States. Offering absolutely no assistance, the prosecutor informed Andrea that if Rosa was no longer in the country, charges would be dropped, for the accused has the right to face his accuser. Andrea now faced a deadline of bringing Rosa back to the United States from Guatemala, a country where Andrea had never been, with a language Andrea did not speak. Without a second thought, she bought a plane ticket for herself and a translator and was on her way to find Rosa.

Upon arrival in Guatemala, Andrea began searching for Rosa. She had heard Ana and Rosa speak of their home village, and after asking around, Andrea discovered that she would need to travel to a mountainous village over eight hours away. Andrea found a driver who was willing to make the treacherous journey with her and the translator. The trip was eight hours of winding mountain roads with no safety barriers to protect the rickety jeep from falling over the edge. When the traveling crew reached the village, Andrea discovered why an offer to Rosa and Ana to leave the village by a trafficker would be difficult to resist. The homes were tents, there was no running water, and the family of fourteen fed on a daily diet of homemade corn tortillas and coffee.

Rosa was thrilled to see Andrea. They discussed a plan for getting Rosa a new passport so that she could return to the United States. Andrea had been told that all that was needed was Rosa's signature and her fingerprints, so Andrea, Rosa, the translator, and the driver drove another eight hours down the mountain to apply for a new passport. When they reached the agency, they learned there was a completely different application process. What would be needed was at least one biological parent to sign the application in person at the agency. Without hesitation, the driver turned to Andrea and said "Let's go!" The four travelers once again began the treacherous journey back up the mountain.

Rosa's mother was more than willing to travel to the city to help her daughter. She left her twelve young children unattended, climbed into the jeep, and the five went back down the mountain. By this time the agency was closed, and so Rosa, her mother, Andrea, and the translator found a hotel in the city for the night.

The next morning, the three went to the agency and applied for the passport. While waiting, Andrea had the unfortunate battle of trying to get plane tickets back to the United States on Thanksgiving. Though it was a seemingly impossible task, Andrea managed to book a flight that would have Rosa back in the United States the day after Thanksgiving, which was also the last day the prosecutor would wait before dropping the charges against the foster father. As the prosecutorial deadline was approaching, Rosa received her official passport, and Andrea and Rosa began their travel back to the United States.

Once back in the States, Andrea and Rosa made their way to the prosecutor's office. Slack-jawed, the prosecutor agreed to go forward with the trial—a trial that would eventually last two years. The foster father was found guilty of sexual assault and sentenced to ten years in prison. Andrea told me that ten years was nothing compared to the torture he had put Rosa through, but it was evidence that victims of human trafficking are not disposable peoples and will be protected by the law. However, that protection is slim and would not have been fulfilled if it had not been for the persistence of Andrea.

Today, Rosa has been granted a T visa. She completed nursing school and has now decided to return to college to pursue a medical degree. Ana is also completing college, and has a beautiful son. The sisters are still in touch with Andrea, giving her constant updates on their lives. Although Andrea is humble in her own efforts, she is haunted by the reality confessed to her by Rosa: before Andrea made it to the village, Rosa was planning to commit suicide, but wanted to be sure that her younger siblings would not be the ones to find her. Andrea saved Rosa in more ways than one, and the tears in her eyes told me that there is nothing she would have done differently.

I was told this story by Andrea in a small office in Ft. Myers, Florida. This was the first time we had met, and I was amazed that my research would take me to such a powerful and dedicated woman. She is a constant advocate for victims of human trafficking, and takes every measure to make sure that victims who have been identified are protected to her fullest ability. Andrea is one of many local advocates in the Immokalee area who are dedicated to identifying and protecting victims. While there are a number of advocacy groups that fight against human trafficking in the United States, this chapter will identify three prominent groups that focus specifically on human trafficking in southern Florida. These groups are the Human Trafficking Task Force spearheaded through Zonta International, Catholic Charities' human trafficking program, and the Coalition of Immokalee Workers (CIW). This is by no means an exhaustive list of the groups and individuals that are working to end slavery in Immokalee, but it is representative of the various missions and the obstacles with which advocacy groups are confronted.

Human Trafficking Awareness Taskforce

In 2004, a small group of women decided to embark on the mission of evaluating the true scope of human trafficking in southwestern Florida. These women were part of the larger organization known as Zonta, which is "a global organization of executives and professionals working together to advance the status of women worldwide through service and advocacy" (zonta.org, accessed October 2010). Within a few months, the small group of women hosted their first human trafficking informational meeting with law enforcement, services providers, and community based organizations. Amazingly, this meeting would lead to the arrest of four traffickers.

Nola Theiss, executive director of the Human Trafficking Awareness Taskforce, explained that at the initial meeting, the various participants began to discuss the signals associated with a trafficked victim. During this discussion, a social worker attending the meeting became aware that a young girl in her foster home met the criteria of a trafficked victim. The victim was described as a young Guatemalan girl who had been enslaved as a domestic servant and a sex slave who was passed from man to man. The young girl became pregnant, and six months into her pregnancy, her handler punched her in the stomach. The woman of the house released her and the young girl was sent to the hospital. The police were called, but their own biases made them less than helpful. Department of Child and Family Services (DCFS) was also called, and the social worker felt it would be safest to send the young girl back home (to her trafficker). Eventually she was placed in a foster home across the street from her handler, and for the following three years, the young girl floated from home to home. It is clear that the girl would still be trapped as an unidentified trafficked victim caught up in foster care if this social worker had not been attending this informational meeting. Today the young girl has been granted a T visa, and as already stated, four traffickers were arrested. Two years after this initial meeting, in 2006, the Human Trafficking Awareness Taskforce was officially founded.

As stated on the Taskforce's website, "Because human trafficking is a hidden crime which can only be eradicated by an informed public, supporting professional law enforcement, and service providers," it is necessary to educate all community groups.[3] The mission of the Taskforce is to build awareness, help community groups organize, share resources with organizations, share information from research, and create prevention programs. Ms. Theiss was especially proud of the newest prevention program that had recently been developed. This program is identified as prevention through art, a program known as ARTREACH. Young girls in southern Florida attend a seminar in which they learn about human trafficking. After the training, with the assistance of an art therapist, the girls create various paintings in relation to human trafficking; some of the girls illustrate their own experience as victims. The objectives of this project are:

> To educate girls about the dangers of human trafficking, the statistics and facts concerning human trafficking and be given the background of the occurrence of human trafficking...; To assist the girls in the creation of four canvas wall hangings which will express their knowledge and understanding of modern-day slavery, especially as it potentially affects their peer group; To bring girls from different backgrounds together to share their knowledge, talent and understanding; To exhibit, display and reproduce the artwork to build awareness of the crime and to interest others in this issue; and To create a template of this project which can be shared with other communities which may wish to replicate this project (ibid).

This artwork has been displayed throughout southern Florida as a unique form of awareness and education.

"Lucia's Letter" is another resource extended to interested parties. Lucia's Letter is the true account of a young Guatemalan girl's journey to the United States in the hands of a trafficker. Her story "is told as a warning to other young women and their mothers not to send their daughters away in the hopes of finding a better life, but rather to educate them to improve life in Guatemala" (ibid). Interested groups may utilize this resource to educate members of their community as well as provide a real-life situation exposing the realities of human trafficking—a scenario that brings the statistics and discussions of trafficking into each person's reality.[4]

The Taskforce does not work directly with victims of trafficking, but rather the members of the Taskforce teach interested parties how to relate to the issues surrounding human trafficking while also persuading them to exert political pressure. The key focus groups are members of the community and community leaders, but the Taskforce has been known to train law enforcement, members of the military, probation officers, paralegals, prosecutors, and various other legal professionals. As stated by Ms. Theiss, "The fight against human trafficking must include all community groups."

As much as the Taskforce emphasizes community involvement, there are still cultural views that create obstacles. For example, the police and legal professionals are more concerned with identifying and prosecuting the trafficker, whereas advocates are focused on identifying and protecting victims. In order to combat these cultural obstacles, the movement has to be perceived as a local community effort. This in and of itself has proved to be problematic, for the efforts employed to combat trafficking have moved from a federal initiative to a local one. When asked about this role reversal, Ms. Theiss reiterated that "both federal and local communities are combating the problem, but there is no funding [available for the local advocates]. Human trafficking must be combated at all levels, not just the local level." A third obstacle confronted by the Taskforce is the rotation of various law officers in charge of the departments associated with human trafficking. This is problematic in that with each new face of the law, the victims take a step backward in the level of trust. The trust between law officers and victims is crucial to eradicating human trafficking. Therefore, Ms. Theiss stated that the "key thing for law enforcement to be effective is to be continuous. [A] core group of same individuals [should be] maintained." Despite the various dilemmas and cultural obstacles, the Taskforce continues to help as many people as possible to organize and coordinate awareness.

In its four years of existence, the Taskforce has achieved various accomplishments. According to Ms. Theiss, the Taskforce has trained twenty-five communities, fifteen of which have a strong local effort to fight human trafficking. Currently, these local efforts have approximately fifty people involved, twenty of whom are actively involved. The Taskforce has also had an invitation to organize a group of community leaders in South Africa, making the Taskforce an international effort against human trafficking.

Catholic Charities, Ft. Myers, Florida

Catholic Charities of Ft. Myers, Florida has an intimate relationship with the previously discussed Human Trafficking Task Force in that both groups work closely with the sheriff's office and the assistant US district attorney in being the "human trafficking informants." The key difference between the two organizations is that where the Human Trafficking Task Force has the mission to educate the public to identify victims of trafficking, Catholic Charities actually provides services to them. An unfortunate similarity between the two organizations is that there exist a number of obstacles that Catholic Charities must confront in order to maintain a safe environment for victims of trafficking.

In 2002, Mary Lewis, a coordinator of the human trafficking program through Catholic Charities, was running a home for teenage mothers and their children. This home, known as Mother's Home, became the refuge for a number of trafficked girls who had been rescued or escaped from a life of rape and forced prostitution. In an interesting twist of fate, it was Ms. Lewis who had attended that first meeting of the Human Trafficking Taskforce and identified the young girl from Guatemala as a victim of trafficking. This young girl happened to be living with Ms. Lewis at the time of that first meeting. It was this moment that altered Ms. Lewis' route toward one of victim identification and protection.

According to my conversation with Ms. Lewis, the mission of the human trafficking program is to "protect and to help the victim to become self-actualized and give them what they need to survive." This mission is fulfilled through housing, education, counseling, and victim assistance. According to the federal mandate, Catholic Charities may assist victims of trafficking only if they are attempting to work with law enforcement (unless the victim is under the age of eighteen), which has proven to be problematic for the program due to the fact that a number of young women and girls are in need of protection and assistance, but they are too fearful to confront their trafficker. Because Catholic Charities has been a recipient of federal trafficking grants to fund services provided to victims, the advocates must abide the mandate in order to receive future funding.

A significant obstacle with which the human trafficking program is confronted is the local community. According to Ms. Lewis, "The public is in denial. Our community is not wanting to have to deal with it. It messes up the way they think." As with other communities throughout the country, it is difficult for the public to face the reality that something as horrific as modern-day slavery is actually occurring in their own back yard. Therefore, aside from victim assistance, the human trafficking program has taken on the secondary task of community outreach, which includes public speaking, community service, and presentations. Unlike the Human Trafficking Task Force, Catholic Charities only provides public outreach initiatives within their host county. Because the community is likely to ignore the reality of trafficking, the program endorses constant awareness and education.

According to Ms. Lewis, an even more considerable obstacle for all anti-trafficking advocates is the sheer size of the human trafficking organization. Ms. Lewis was quite truthful when she argued that "we are not going to eradicate it. They are bigger than we are; we are up against some huge, powerful organization." Therefore, the human trafficking program has not made any attempt or promise to completely eradicate human trafficking in their community. Rather, they keep their focus very specific. For the program, saving one person is evidence that something is being done to reduce the problem of trafficking.

The work of Catholic Charities is not conducted in a vacuum. The organization works closely with local law enforcement. This seems to be a unique relationship because most nonprofit organizations do not work in conjunction with law enforcement. However, there seems to be "mutual respect" between law enforcement and the human trafficking program. The goals may be different in that law enforcement has the central mission to "catch the bad guy," versus the goal of victim protection held by anti-trafficking advocates, but the end result remains the same: reducing human trafficking in the local community. As with the Human Trafficking Task Force, the human trafficking program recognizes the federal-local disconnect, but to Ms. Lewis, the fight against human trafficking "has to be a local issue." Although there is a preference for federal involvement, the disparities in the penalty phase of the law create too much confusion in the prosecutorial phase of the anti-trafficking efforts. Therefore, as with the Task Force, Catholic Charities recognizes that in order to partake in anti-trafficking initiatives, the efforts are to be local. More importantly, these local efforts must include forcing the community to recognize and participate in anti-trafficking efforts.

Today, the human trafficking taskforce of Catholic Charities has developed into a reputable resource for victims of trafficking. The program receives calls from case management, social workers, and emergency workers, and members of the local community seeking educational outreach and/or victim protection. As stated by the assistant US district attorney, advocates of the Task Force have assisted in the prosecution of over twenty cases as well as the freeing over fifty victims of trafficking in the past decade. These efforts are immeasurable in the lives that have been saved, and the lives that are yet to be identified. However, a striking absence in the work of the Task Force and Catholic Charities is that the victims they identify and protect are predominantly women and children forced into commercial sexual slavery; those enslaved in the fields are not the core initiatives of the two groups. However, there is one advocate movement that has the sole mission of improving the lives of the fieldworkers in Immokalee: The Coalition of Immokalee Workers (CIW).

Coalition of Immokalee Workers

No other Immokalee advocate group has been more researched or more publicized than the CIW. Founded in the early 1990s, the Coalition has been on the front lines in improving the work conditions of the enslaved tomato pickers. With its widespread popularity, the Coalition leaders are somewhat private in divulging any information that may be misconstrued, and for that reason they denied all interview attempts from this "strange author" from the Midwest. Therefore, the material regarding the Coalition comes second-hand from authors who were able to talk to Coalition leaders and from the Coalition's own website, www.ciw-online.org.

The most prominent mission of the CIW has been to increase field laborers' salaries so that they may earn a fair wage. In 1993, a small group of farmworkers began to conduct weekly meetings in a church to determine how they could generate public pressure to increase their sub-poverty wages, while at the same time improving the life conditions of their small community. By means of statewide marches and a well-documented hunger strike, the small group was able to draw the public's attention to the plight of the farmworkers. As stated proudly on the Coalition's website: "By 1998 we had won industry-wide raises of 13–25% (translating into several million dollars annually for the community in increased wages) and a new-found political and social respect from the outside world." Although this was an astounding victory in the short five years of organizing, the leaders of the Coalition recognized that the struggle against the large corporations that continued to oppress the field workers was far from over.

Currently, the Coalition has two other missions to add to their fair wage campaign: an anti-slavery campaign and a campaign for fair food. In conjunction with students and community advocates, the anti-slavery campaign has generated much attention from national media outlets such as National Public Radio (NPR). Unlike the other advocate groups discussed in this chapter, the anti-slavery campaign is focused on eliminating agricultural slavery, first and foremost in Immokalee and surrounding Florida communities, but also on a national scale. As highlighted on their website, "the CIW helps fight this crime [of agricultural slavery] by uncovering, investigating, and assisting in the federal prosecution of slavery rings preying on hundreds of farmworkers," and their work has proven successful. In fact, in a decade's time, the CIW has assisted in the successful prosecutions of at least six different slave rings in Florida (see Table 5.1).

Table 5.1: Successful Prosecutions of Traffickers

U.S. vs. Flores — In 1997, Miguel Flores and Sebastian Gomez were sentenced to 15 years each in federal prison on slavery, extortion, and firearms charges, among others. Flores and Gomez had a workforce of over 400 men and women in Florida and South Carolina, harvesting vegetables and citrus. The workers, mostly indigenous Mexicans and Guatemalans, were forced to work 10–12-hour days, 6 days per week, for as little as $20 per week, under the watch of armed guards. Those who attempted escape were assaulted, pistol-whipped, and even shot. The case was brought to federal authorities after five years of investigation by escaped workers and CIW members.

U.S. vs. Cuello — In 1999, Abel Cuello was sentenced to 33 months in federal prison on slavery charges. He had held more than 30 tomato pickers in two trailers in the isolated swampland west of Immokalee, keeping them under constant watch. Three workers escaped the camp, only to have their boss track them down a few weeks later. The employer ran one of them down with his car, stating that he owned them. The workers sought help from the CIW and the police, and the CIW worked with the DOJ on the ensuing investigation. Cuello worked for Manley Farms North, Inc., a major Bonita Springs tomato supplier. Once out of prison, Cuello supplied labor to Ag-Mart Farms, a tomato company operating in Florida and North Carolina.

U.S. vs. Tecum — In 2001, Jose Tecum was sentenced to 9 years in federal prison on slavery and kidnapping charges. He forced a young woman to work against her will both in the tomato fields around Immokalee, and in his home. The CIW assisted the DOJ with the prosecution, including victim and witness assistance.

U.S. vs. Lee — In 2001, Michael Lee was sentenced to 4 years in federal prison and 3 years supervised release on a slavery conspiracy charge. He pled guilty to using crack cocaine, threats, and violence to enslave his workers. Lee held his workers in forced labor, recruiting homeless U.S. citizens for his operation, creating a "company store" debt through loans for rent, food, cigarettes, and cocaine. He abducted and beat one of his workers to prevent him from leaving his employ. Lee harvested for orange growers in the Fort Pierce, FL, area.

U.S. vs. Ramos — In 2004, Ramiro and Juan Ramos were sentenced to 15 years each in federal prison on slavery and firearms charges, and the forfeiture of over $3 million in assets. The men, who had a workforce of over 700 farmworkers in the citrus groves of Florida, as well as the fields of North Carolina, threatened workers with death if they were to try to leave, and pistol-whipped and assaulted — at gunpoint — passenger van service drivers who gave rides to farmworkers leaving the area. The case was brought to trial by the DOJ after two years of investigation by the CIW. The Ramoses harvested for Consolidated Citrus and Lykes Brothers, among others.

U.S. vs. Ronald Evans — In 2007, Florida employer Ron Evans was sentenced to 30 years in federal prison on drug conspiracy, financial restructuring, and witness tampering charges, among others. Jequita Evans was also sentenced to 20 years, and Ron Evans Jr. to 10 years. Operating in Florida and North Carolina, Ron Evans recruited homeless U.S. citizens from shelters across the Southeast, including New Orleans, Tampa, and Miami, with promises of good jobs and housing. At Palatka, FL, and Newton Grove, NC, area labor camps, the Evanses deducted rent, food, crack cocaine, and alcohol from workers' pay, holding them "perpetually indebted" in what the DOJ called "a form of servitude morally and legally reprehensible." The Palatka labor camp was surrounded by a chain link fence topped with barbed wire, with a No Trespassing sign. The CIW and a Miami-based homeless outreach organization (Touching Miami with Love) began the investigation and reported the case to federal authorities in 2003. In Florida, Ron Evans worked for grower Frank Johns. Johns was 2004 Chairman of the Florida Fruit and Vegetable Association, the powerful lobbying arm of the Florida agricultural industry. As of 2007, he remained the Chairman of the FFVA's Budget and Finance Committee.

(Information derived from ciw-online.org)

Aside from the federal prosecutions, the CIW has brought nationwide attention to the modern-day slavery evident in Immokalee and surrounding community, as well as assisting to provide the freedom to "more than a thousand tomato and orange pickers held in debt bondage."

The other pertinent mission of the CIW is the campaign for fair food. Again, through the use of media outlets and student organizations, the CIW has generated much publicity on the "penny more per pound" campaign. Going after large corporations such as Taco Bell, Burger King, Chipotle, and Publix grocery store, the members of the CIW demand that these companies increase their payment for tomatoes one more cent per pound. If company leaders refuse to increase the pay, members and supporters of the CIW partake in a disparaging protest compelling citizens to refuse to support slavery by boycotting the noncompliant businesses. Some recent victories of the penny-more-per-pound campaign include agreements with Taco Bell (2005), McDonalds (2007), and Burger King (2008). In August 2010, the Sodexo corporation became one of the newest members to sign the campaign for fair food agreement. Unfortunately, a number of industries have yet to sign the agreement, and so the penny-more-per-pound mission continues.

Currently, the CIW claims over three thousand members, mostly farmworkers of Mexican, Guatemalan, and Haitian descent. "Joining costs ten dollars and, technically, entails little more than receiving a photo ID" (Bowe 2007: 24). Although the membership consists of what has been deemed a disposable population in the United States, the movement has gained both national and global recognition. For example, in September 2010, CIW leader Romeo Ramirez won a video contest publicizing human rights violations in the United States. The award for this contest was an engagement for Ramirez to address UN Human Rights Council in Geneva, Switzerland in November 2010. Laura Germino, one of the movement's anti-slavery campaign leaders, was honored by U.S. Secretary of State Hillary Clinton for her efforts to eradicate modern-day slavery in the United States. Additionally, a number of political actors, including former President Jimmy Carter, Florida Governor Charles Crist, and Illinois Senator Dick Durbin, have expressed immense support for the movement. The CIW prides itself on how a small group of farmworkers meeting in a church in Immokalee, Florida, have transformed into a forceful presence bringing national and international attention to modern-day slavery in the agricultural fields of the United States.

Despite its growth in membership, recognition, and power, the CIW continues to face obstacles to the ultimate mission of eradicating slavery. Perhaps the greatest obstacle to the movement is the same that was identified by Ms. Lewis of Catholic Charities: the general public. As the story at the introduction of this chapter illustrated, it is very difficult for the members of the CIW to spread their message beyond the borders of Immokalee. Until the public consciousness can be altered to realize that the food on their dinner table was a product of modern-day slavery, the pressure will remain at a plateau, for the CIW can only exert so much pressure on the farm owners. The most recent attempt of the movement to increase awareness is its participation in the slavery museum that has traveled throughout the Northeast. This museum attracted citizens throughout the country, bringing awareness to the history of slavery in the United States, as well as the presence of modern-day slavery evident in Florida and other agricultural communities.

Aside from public awareness of the issue of slavery, the farm owners in and of themselves will remain a great limitation to the eradication of slavery. As the assistant US district attorney explained, the problem is not being able to prosecute the actual growers due to the line of ignorance that is created between the grower and the pit-bosses and contractors. As growers continues to deny any knowledge of what their field bosses are doing to the farmworkers, they claim they have no responsibility and therefore cannot be prosecuted. As the assistant US district attorney explained to me:

> The minute that I am able to prove a case against a grower is the minute that the system changes. I see a lot of growers blame it on their pit bosses or their field bosses—in Florida that is the convenient way to do it. But, just like in any drug organization, if you flip a middle man up, or you have somebody undercover, then that grower gets arrested. Now, there are a lot of good growers out there—there's a lot of people who try to play by the rules and hate the ones that are not playing by the rules because it undercuts their money. But the minute a farmer finds out about his fellow farmer being arrested, all of a sudden he is going to call in his field boss and he'll say "I don't feel like going to jail, so your job has just changed."

Unless this chain of events occurs, the growers are going to conduct business in a way that bypasses international human rights standards so that they may generate capital.

Although the future looks bleak if the change is dependent on the growers, the CIW has been able to persuade a number of industries to assist in improving the conditions in the field by urging corporate leaders to agree to pay the surcharge of a penny-more-per-pound. For example, in 2001, the CIW launched its penny-more-per-pound campaign against Taco Bell, and after years of consistent protest, Taco Bell finally agreed to pay the penny surcharge, paving the way for optimistic protest by the CIW against other large food corporations. The agreement exemplified the importance of networking, for the victory was partially the result of University student groups protesting the campus branches of Taco Bell. It is important to reiterate that a number of the CIW victories both past and present have been the result of the advocates networking with influential community members as well as educating the public through peaceful protests. Although the CIW is a powerful force, the validity of consumer dissatisfaction has historically been an effective negotiating strategy.

The successful effort to persuade Taco Bell to pay a penny more per pound of tomatoes was just the beginning of victories for the CIW. Beginning in 2005, the CIW, once again in alignment with student groups, set their focus on McDonalds in the penny-more-per-pound campaign. After two years of letter writing and public protests, the CIW claimed another victory when McDonalds signed the agreement in 2007. However, the 2007 victory against McDonalds met with hostility from the Florida Tomato Grower's Exchange, which threatened to fine any farmer that participated in or supported the CIW's campaign. However, the CIW did not falter; in 2007 it launched another campaign, this time targeting Burger King. Within one year, Burger King had agreed to pay the surcharge. Additionally, in 2008, Whole Foods grocery stores and Subway restaurants signed the agreement to pay the surcharge.

After the victories with Burger King, Subway, and Whole Foods, the CIW began urging more supermarkets to pay the surcharge, specifically targeting Publix, Kroger, Ahold, and Trader Joe's. At the time of this writing, not one of these supermarket chains has signed the surcharge agreement. On the other hand, in 2010 the CIW achieved perhaps of the greatest victories when Pacific Tomato Growers agreed to distribute a surcharge to the farmworkers of a penny more per pound. Partners of Pacific Tomato publicly made the announcement of the new surcharge in the hope that it would "encourage other growers to help end abuses of workers" (Perez 2010). This victory has set the stage for a new level of advocacy to begin, for a tomato growing organization has opened a door for other growers to support the surcharge campaign. Although there have been pitfalls and obstacles against the CIW, the first part of the twenty-first century indicates that the CIW is a powerful front with the ability to change the behaviors of restaurant owners, grocery chains, and members of the tomato growing industry. It appears that the CIW has reached a crossroads where real change will emerge for the farmworkers of Immokalee, Florida.

Immokalee in the Community and Media

While a large part of society presents a backlash to undocumented workers despite their victimized status (see Chapter 2), members of the surrounding community and local media seem to sympathize strongly with the highly publicized tomato workers. Some reference was given to the women trapped in sexual slavery, but overall, there seemed to be awareness of the oppressiveness of the tomato industry. For example, while sitting in a bar in Naples one evening, I began to discuss my research with the bar staff. The two tending bar immediately spoke of support for my research, claiming that what was occurring was "so sad" and that "something needs to be done to help these workers." In addition, there was consensus that the statuses of the workers were overshadowed by their victimization. The servers stated an unconcern as how the farmworkers came to the United States, and expressed an interest in assisting the victims, whether through contributing to advocacy groups or protesting the industry by purchasing only homegrown tomatoes.

Other members of the community I spoke with shared a similar passion to assist the farmworkers. Although they had not joined any sort of movement, they were pleased to hear that I planned to publicize the plight of the Immokalee slaves in a book. In fact, one friend I met in my travels told me that he would like me to let him know when the book came out so that he could be sure to have it stocked in the independent bookstore. He believed that the issue needed to be more present in the community, and would do what he could to help publicize the inhumanities occurring in the nearby town. Many individuals I spoke with agreed that this was an important topic to be exposed and that the workers need their voice to be heard. From Naples to Ft. Myers Beach, most everyone with whom I had a conversation, whether hotel clerks, restaurant workers, or shopkeepers, seemed to have knowledge of the Immokalee workers and readily spoke to me about their dissatisfaction with the tomato industry.

The local media was just as responsive as the neighboring communities in presenting a sympathetic view for the undocumented workers of Immokalee. When I first began this research, I was sought out by a local newsman who wished to gain my perspective from my first round of interviews (Cornwell 2009). His article presented the background information of Immokalee, the current level of slavery in the fields, and the response of the local police and advocates, all of whom he referred to as heroes. In addition, he attempted to absolve the stereotypes associated with Immokalee, presenting a town of history and hope. This story was unique to the discussion of Immokalee, for the town itself is usually not highlighted in the everyday media. Rather, when stories are published, they are usually in response to a new investigation or prosecution. Given this, the discussion is not on illegal immigration, but instead the victimization associated with human trafficking.

Interestingly, both in the media and through my casual conversations, the focus was on the tomato fields. Some media pieces would discuss the sex trafficking rings, but this was only if a brothel had been identified or a prosecution had just been successful. This is distinct from the national discussion of trafficking, in that most of the research focuses on the sexual servitude aspect, often dedicating very little discussion to labor trafficking, specifically agricultural slavery. The surrounding communities of Immokalee are fully aware of the agricultural slavery, yet seem to be less well informed about the sexual servitude also evident in the small town. Despite the half-sighted awareness, neighboring communities and local media presented to me an overall acceptance of the workers and sympathized with their substandard work and living conditions.

Conclusion

Although the three organizations discussed in this chapter have provided invaluable assistance to the local police in Immokalee, as well in the prosecution of slavery cases, not always have the advocates and legal professionals seen eye to eye. According to the assistant US district attorney:

> There is one case [when] we raided a brothel. Two [women in the brothel] were obviously slaves. We put them in a nongovernmental organization, and when we went around to interview them the next Monday, they were gone, because the organization, who shall remain nameless, put them on a bus back to Mexico so they wouldn't have to be revictimized, thereby taking [the] case right along with them.

This case is illustrative of the different missions of the NGOs, as well as how their efforts impact the overall prosecution of the slavery. Although members of the NGOs work with the police and prosecutors, their mission is to protect the victim, not oblige the legal actors. As mentioned in the previous chapter, much of the time in Immokalee, the CIW and the local police do not agree, for their missions are not always be the same. Therefore, if advocates believe that a victim would be safer without confronting the attacker, or fear that the victim of a trafficking situation will be deported if after identifying it, the advocates will remove the victim from the reach of legal actors. Prosecuting the offender is not the concern of the advocates. Although it is admirable to work so fervently on behalf of the victim, the legal actors believe that these actions are a huge obstacle to the punishment of the trafficker, which is the legal mission.

The conflicting interests between members of NGOs and the legal actors are a problem not just in Immokalee, but nationwide. In some cases, the discord is so great that the advocates refuse to work with the local police and prosecutors. Therefore, the issue becomes who is right in their cause, rather than what can we do to protect the victims of human trafficking? Advocates and legal actors across the country may learn from the Immokalee example that missions may conflict, but the focus should always be on identifying the victim, and then prosecuting the slaver while empowering the victim throughout the process. This is only possible through networking and understanding the unique role of each organization involved in the process of eradicating human trafficking in each community.

As this chapter has illustrated, nongovernmental organizations nationwide are essential in the battle against human trafficking. Many of the members are everyday citizens who have heard about trafficking at a taskforce meeting or on the local media and have decided to advocate on behalf of the victims in their own community. In some cases, the members of the advocacy-based group were once part of the victim community they are now fighting to protect, as with the CIW. The members of nongovernmental organizations are willing to see the victims and take responsibility for them once identified. The advocates discussed in this chapter are true believers in their struggle against trafficking, and maintain the focus that their work is for the victim. There are always problems associated with advocacy-based work, including the possibility of becoming too political or changing the mission to appease bureaucratic leaders, but the groups highlighted in this chapter have stayed true to their mission. Therefore, we may learn from the efforts of the advocates discussed in this chapter in that nongovernmental organizations are crucial in the battle against human trafficking in the United States. The identification of victims and successful prosecutions could not be possible without the assistance of advocates. These individuals are often invisible to our everyday consciousness, but their voices are loud, and their efforts are immeasurable to the victims that they have assisted. As one advocate so eloquently put it, "It is impossible to identify all victims of human trafficking, but if we are able to help one individual, I consider that a success."

The African proverb, "When spider webs unite, they can tie up a lion," is quite relevant to the efforts made by advocates in the struggle against modern-day slavery and human trafficking. Groups of everyday citizens have embarked on the extraordinary undertaking of identifying and protecting victims, while assisting law enforcement and prosecutors in the punishment of the traffickers. Together, these individuals become a powerful force on the frontline of a seemingly impossible battle. Perhaps, though, the system can be altered as cooperation is increased and the reality is stressed that the battle against modern-day slavery and human trafficking is a local effort, and must be fought and won in the local arena.

[1] The Penny More per Pound campaign is the sole mission of the CIW in which they demand large companies to pay a penny more per pound of tomatoes so that the workers may earn a more livable wage.

[2] The names have been changed to protect the privacy of the individuals.

[3] humantraffickingawareness.org, accessed 2010

[4] To read a copy of Lucia's letter, visit: http://www.wgcu.org/Lucia-s-Letter

6

Effecting Change

"As I would not be a slave, so I would not be a master."
—Abraham Lincoln

The many factors associated with human trafficking often create a complex web of uncertainties. Throughout this book, I have described the conditions of slavery and what measures have been taken at the local level to improve the livelihood of identified victims. However, I am quite certain that the reader has more questions than answers—perhaps more than when they began reading this book. "What can I do?" "Can trafficking be stopped?" These questions, along with many more, are what I have asked myself, as well as what I have been asked. However, I do not have all of the answers. Rather, I have ideas; and perhaps, to continue in the battle against trafficking, ideas are the strongest weapon. Therefore, the purpose of the conclusion to this book is not to provide the reader with the answers to the multiple questions surrounding the issues of trafficking and modern-day slavery, but rather to focus on the changes in Immokalee and what steps can be done to reduce the demand that fuels trafficking in the United States. As has been stated throughout the book, I believe, just as do the advocates and local police, that human trafficking cannot be eradicated. At the same time, I believe that small actions by everyday citizens can improve the life conditions of some of those who have been trafficked and are forced into a system of slavery. I am hopeful for a better future in Immokalee, yet many of the changes that have occurred in the past year have made for new obstacles in the battle against human trafficking.

The "New" Immokalee

Over the years, the landscape of Immokalee has remained relatively stable. Some houses continue to crumble, weeds grow from inches into feet, and workers wander the streets or sit under the warm sun on the days when they have not been able to find work. As the background appears to be the same year after year, new changes in the avenues of assistance have heightened concern among the advocates and some of the legal bodies as they attempt to continue their mission to identify and protect victims of trafficking while punishing the offenders. The most crucial of these changes has been the election of a new governor in the state of Florida.

When I first began investigating slavery in Immokalee, the governor of state at that time was Charles Crist. Through letter writing campaigns and public protests, the CIW had been putting pressure on Crist to acknowledge the agricultural slavery in Immokalee. After years during which the governor avoided the CIW, the advocates finally got through to Crist, and he eventually became a crusader against human trafficking and agricultural slavery. In a letter to the CIW, Crist expressed the following:

> The information [the CIW] provided greater expanded my understanding of the hardships the workers face while enduring this difficult employment. I have no tolerance for slavery in any form, and I am committed to eliminating this injustice anywhere in Florida. I unconditionally support the humane and civilized treatment of all employees, including those who work in Florida's agricultural industry. Any type of abuse in the workplace is unacceptable. (Quoted in Maxwell 2009)

Crist was the first Florida governor to speak out against slave labor in the state, and more importantly, he took a proactive stance by joining the CIW's fair food campaign demanding a penny more per pound.

Although he did not take into account the sexual slavery evident in Immokalee, Crist did make a strong attempt to improve the living conditions by demanding that the Tomato Growers Exchange join the effort in providing the farmworkers an extra penny per pound of tomatoes picked. At the time of this writing, the Growers Exchange, which represents 90 percent of the state's tomato growers, has not budged in its position of providing the workers more money, and "has implemented a $100,000 fine for any member that pays workers extra" (ibid.).

In November 2010, Governor Rick Scott took office in Florida, and he has not had such a supportive relationship with the CIW. In fact, Governor Scott has taken a strong stance against immigration, proposing that Florida adopt an immigration law based on the Arizona immigration law SB 1070. According to Scott, "If you're stopped in our state—no different than if you're asked for your ID—you should be able to be asked if you're legal or not" (Wing 2010). The difference between the proposed immigration enforcement and the current 287(g) program is that under 287(g), officers may ask for the status of an immigrant only after an arrest has been made. If Florida moves toward Arizona-style immigration enforcement, officers may ask the status of an individual during any sort of "legitimate contact" where the officer feels "reasonable suspicion exists that the person is an alien who is unlawfully present in the U.S." (Arizona, SB 1070, 2010). In other words, there is the very real threat of racial profiling on the part of officers in determining the status of individuals in Immokalee.

In addition to the threat of racial profiling, the proposed legislation would necessitate the immediate removal of undocumented immigrants in the United States. This is especially problematic in human trafficking cases, for victims may be deported without receiving the services needed to alleviate their victimization. Many of the victims suffer from psychological and physical trauma, but these symptoms will be disregarded as they are returned to their country of origin. Once sent back, victims once again become vulnerable to the issues associated with poverty, such as hunger, exploitation, and sexual oppression. Additionally, despite their dire situation in the States, many of the victims were under the illusion that they would experience freedom once their debt was repaid. Therefore, many of the unidentified victims of trafficking who are deported due to immigration status are likely to take the risk of reentering the United States, usually with the assistance of a trafficker. Thus the cycle continues, and authorities have done very little to protect the victims of trafficking.

In addition to the maintenance of trafficking, immediate deportation also places the victim's family at risk. As stated throughout the book, a tool of psychological restraint is threatening victims and their families. Once the victim is returned to the country of origin, this threat becomes a reality. Regardless of how the victim returned home, the trafficker is left with an unpaid debt. To save face, and to keep other victims from "escaping through deportation," victims and their families face a very real risk of bodily harm or murder. Unless the family or the victim can earn the funds to pay the trafficker's fees, which is highly unlikely, the family is left with very few options; these include returning the victim to the trafficker, or attempting to escape through methods other than using a trafficker or smuggler.

Immediate deportation also affects the process of prosecution. All successful trafficking prosecutions have in part depended on the victim's assistance and testimony. If a trafficker has been identified but victims have been deported, the prosecutor must build a case on evidence alone, without the assistance and compelling testimony of a victim. Even if the prosecutor hopes to bring the victim back to the United States for purposes of prosecution, finding the victim is relatively impossible. Recall the story of Rosa discussed in Chapter 3. Although Rosa was not legally deported from the United States, her forced return to Guatemala would have made her appearance at the trial impossible had it not been for extraordinary efforts made by one local advocate. The actions of the advocate are considered rare in the context of what a typical individual would do in attempting to locate a trafficked victim who had been deported. Although it is possible that similar efforts may be made for a successful prosecution of a trafficker, it is not probable, thereby limiting the evidence and testimony the prosecutor so desperately needs for a successful prosecution.

The election of Governor Scott and the coinciding discussion of the introduction of an Arizona-style immigration enforcement policy in Florida is not the only critical change that will undoubtedly affect the trafficked victims of Immokalee. In June 2010, President Barack Obama nominated Robert E. O'Neill as the United States Attorney for the Middle District of Florida; O'Neill was officially sworn into office in October of 2010. One of O'Neill's first initiatives was to restructure the management team of the state's attorney's office, which resulted in the demotion of the chief assistant US attorney to assistant attorney.[1] This demotion occurred in November 2010. Whereas the once chief assistant US attorney had the supervisory role and corresponding political platform to speak out against and educate the public on issues of trafficking, his responsibilities now rest solely on prosecuting.

Although the assistant US attorney is still capable of prosecuting trafficking cases, the structural change within the states attorney's office has limited the primacy of human trafficking. Prior to the demotion, the former chief assistant US attorney had "become an expert in human trafficking, speaking across the country on the topic after prosecuting cases, many dealing with farm worker abuse in Collier County" (Gillespie 2010: A1). Because he no longer holds the supervisory role, human trafficking cases may not be considered a chief objective of the state's attorney's office. Of course, only time will tell if this summation is accurate; yet with the strong sentiment against undocumented immigrants posited by the governor, it is plausible to believe that human trafficking cases will revert to immigration cases, thereby punishing victims for their status rather than prosecuting traffickers for their offenses against human rights.

While the state's attorney's office was going through a managerial structural change, there was also a transfer of roles at the local level. As I thought of the prospects of writing this book, I reached out to my first contact at the District 8 substation. I wanted to be sure that he was comfortable with the idea of a book and that he was still willing to work with me. I was then told that he had been transferred from his position at the Immokalee substation to another Collier County station. He provided me the contact information of the individual who would be replacing him in Immokalee, who was to become my new contact.

My original contact had some contradictory views regarding the 287(g) program; he believed that only violent felons who disrupted the community should be eligible for deportation. Of course, he also understood the politics associated with his job in local law enforcement, and followed the 287(g) regulations as he was told. Yet, his main initiative was supporting the community and treating victims as victims regardless of their immigration status. He was a proponent of educating the citizens of Immokalee of their rights, and tried to maintain an element of trust between the police and the workers.

My new contact shares similar views—victims are victims regardless of their immigration status—and he hopes to build upon the works of his predecessor. As a long-term member of the Immokalee substation, he does not fear that the restructuring of the district will affect the relationship that has been developed with some of the migrant workers. He also hopes to continue the various missions that are taken on each year to reduce victimization and protect the members of the Immokalee community. However, he is very aware of his responsibilities with respect to enforcing the 287(g) program. Under stricter rules of enforcement, he has explained that there is no incentive to conduct raids or profile members of the community to detect those with undocumented status, but if any member of the Immokalee community is arrested, the status of that individual will be questioned. In accordance with the 287(g) program, if that individual is undocumented, deportation proceedings will begin.

The realization of faithful enforcement under 287(g) is not a new phenomenon created under the structural change within the substation. Yet whether or not the structural change will affect the local officers' perception of the program is unclear. The chilling effect on the part of the officers may be viewed as insubordination, or it may continue just as

138 Sex Slaves and Serfs

it has, undetected if practiced on a small scale. Secondly, although my new contact expresses concern about community initiatives, the missions may become an afterthought in any case due to the difficulties of funding, rules, and other extraneous variables. At the time of this writing, I remain hopeful that the new structure of the Immokalee substation will not affect the overall system of community and trust that has been built upon year after year. Yet this discussion may be null if Governor Scott's proposal for a change in immigration enforcement is actually accepted. If that becomes the case, farmworkers will be more inclined to fear the officers in Immokalee as they have stricter immigration enforcement guidelines to follow. This will lead to distrust and further alienation between the local authorities and the victims of trafficking in Immokalee.

Regardless of the work that has accomplished, many of the undocumented workers are fearful of the immigration enforcement abilities of the local police. Being so, many no longer live in Immokalee, but rather live in what are known as "sanctuary cities."

Sanctuary Cities

"Sanctuary is a term for cities, counties, or states that are defying a federal law relative to the various government agencies being required to assist the federal government with their illegal immigrants" (www.sanctuarycities.info, accessed April 2011). In other words, these cities or states refuse to participate in the 287(g) program by signing the MOAs or statewide immigration enforcement such as in Arizona. Recently, sanctuary cities in Arizona have become controversial; state legislation requires local law enforcement to weed out the illegal element in their cities, but some localities have refused to utilize their resources to enforce immigration law. At this point, this passive protest has not been deemed illegal, but it has raised many questions as to whether or not city enforcement has the right to protest a federal enforcement strategy (see Dinan and Rowland 2010).

Florida has a number of sanctuary cities that have become safe havens for undocumented workers. Although not publicly recognized as such, these cities do not have an MOA with the Department of Homeland Security to enforce immigration law. Therefore, many of the migrant workers and their families are no longer living in Immokalee, but rather in the surrounding cities. The workers are then bussed into the fields to labor for the day, after which they return to their "safe" city. This has created a dilemma for local law enforcement and advocates in Immokalee in that identifying potential trafficking victims is now much more difficult than when the workers were living in town. Because of the limited visibility, it is much easier for traffickers to exploit and oppress victims away from the spying eyes of local enforcement and advocates.

Aside from the mounting difficulty of identifying and consequent protection of victims, having the workers residing outside of Immokalee has created a number of other issues. One of these was discussed in Chapter 2: worker reliance on external networks of support. The workers who do not reside in Immokalee are less likely to participate in CIW meetings and activities, let alone know that such an organization exists. Therefore, these members of the undocumented working class are less likely to receive the protection and benefits associated with membership in the CIW. In addition to the benefits of the CIW, undocumented immigrants may not receive the education offered by local law enforcement, and therefore may not realize that there is relief from victimization if a relationship of trust is developed and maintained between law enforcement, the workers, and their families.

In addition to causing the lack of assistance received by workers and their families living outside of Immokalee, this residential situation actually also impacts the town itself. In the months between October and May, the population of Immokalee once doubled as workers and their families would migrate to the area. As more and more workers have migrated to the cities outside of Immokalee to avoid immigration detection, the overall town has been affected. Structures once serving as work camp housing are now abandoned; these, as discussed in Chapter 3, become vulnerable to brothel activity. Local businesses that cater to the workers are closing, leaving very few options for those workers who still reside in Immokalee. As the town slowly closes down, some question whether Immokalee, the town, will exist twenty years from now, or will it be completely abandoned as more and more workers are bused in from outside the city limits to work the fields.

Sanctuary cities have received praise and criticism from advocates and practitioners alike, but in the case of Immokalee, these "safe places" free from immigration detection may actually cause more harm than good. Advocates and legal professionals trained to identify victims of human trafficking may not be as accessible in sanctuary cities. Similarly, organizations such as the CIW offer services to members of the organizations, as well as identified victims, but if individuals are unaware of the benefits of membership, they may be more vulnerable to exploitation and oppression. Overall, undocumented workers who migrate outside the city limits of Immokalee may be placing themselves at more risk, while at the same time the town itself is potentially disappearing as businesses begin to close and homes become vacant.

The "new" Immokalee is undergoing many changes that will affect the future of identifying and protecting victims of human trafficking. As new political leaders step forward with policy recommendations and previous leaders are demoted or transferred, the future of human trafficking in Immokalee is uncertain. However, as the tomato industry flourishes and sex is commodified, there is a constant risk of human trafficking. Therefore, the efforts toward relative eradication of trafficking must focus on the vulnerability of potential victims, the demand, and what we as citizens are able to do to identify and protect the undocumented workers, women, and children of Immokalee, as well as the entire United States.

Victim Identification and Protection

Perhaps one of the most substantial dilemmas that I came across as I conducted this research was the disparity between the experiences of undocumented workers and victims of sex trafficking and the actions that were/are being taken to reduce victimization. What seems to be occurring is a pluralizing of experiences with a gap where the experiences should overlap. In other words, the legal actors and advocates have presented one story to me as to what actions are being taken to reduce human trafficking in Immokalee. At the same time, slavery in its various forms persists. This is not to say that the efforts made by legal actors and advocates is unimportant, for identifying and protecting one victim is considered an extraordinary victory. Yet, those who remain in the cycle of slavery hardly reap the benefits of identification as they continue to endure their own personal struggle for survival.

Building on a micro-analysis of the victims' experiences, perhaps the first way to protect those caught in the cycle of slavery is to focus on the individual rather than the whole. Throughout this book, I have maintained that no experience is the same as any other, but the similarities of the everyday exploitation lead to a generalizable analysis of modern-day slavery. A problem with my own generalizing of the exploitation is that human trafficking becomes a faceless phenomenon. One of the first steps that ought to be taken by those of us who wish to do more is to start seeing the faces of each victim. An unfortunate aspect of modern culture in the United States is to turn away from that which we do not want to believe. Once we see that human trafficking is not faceless, but rather affects hundreds of thousands of individuals, only then will the severity of the situation truly impact us.

Protecting victims of trafficking is not only dependent on seeing the individuals affected by trafficking; it is also determined by whether or not key identifiers exist. Most victims of human trafficking are not going to voluntarily step forward and identify their own victimization, for within the system of modern slavery exists a culture of fear. As discussed throughout the book, victims and their families are constantly threatened by traffickers as a tool of psychological coercion. Victims will not readily step forward due to the simple fear that they will place themselves or their family in danger. At the same time, there are also other fear-related factors that may inhibit a victim from approaching authorities or advocates. Some of these factors are associated with the economic dependence of the victim on the trafficker, the mistrust of law enforcement, and the perceived stigma associated with being a victim of trafficking. These fears, along with each individual's own personal fear, deter victims from drawing their own victimization to the attention of authorities or advocates. This being so, advocates, legal professionals, social service employees, and concerned citizens alike must look beyond the surface and determine whether some of the crucial identifying markers of victimization exist.

The human trafficking pamphlet (see Appendix B) handed out to migrant workers at the beginning of the harvest season clearly highlights the key indicators of human trafficking. The pamphlet presents the dominant indicators of human trafficking, but some of the identifiers may not be so clearly present. For example, many trafficked workers may not live in close proximity to the work place, nor may some of the listed areas be observed (physical indicators, financial indicators, etc.). Therefore, an individual who believes he or she is in contact with a potential victim of trafficking should consider two additional factors. First of all, if possible, one should find out how much the potential victim was paid. Any payment below the federal minimum standard is an indicator that the individual may be a victim of human trafficking. Secondly, one should attempt to evaluate the level of fear the individual displays, especially in the presence of the employer. The use of threats is a very powerful tool of repression and exploitation, and is deeply intertwined in the system of slavery.

Once identified, a victim may be eligible to receive the benefits of a T visa or "continued presence" if the individual is a victim of a severe form of trafficking; is physically present in the U.S., American Samoa, or Northern Marianas on account of trafficking; has complied with reasonable requests for assistance in investigation or prosecution; and would suffer extreme hardship involving unusual and severe harm upon removal (www.uscis.gov, accessed April 2011). The main difference between a T visa and continued presence is the length of immigration relief (see Table 6.1).

Table 6.1: Continued Presence vs. T Visa[2]

Continued Presence	T Visa
Provides temporary immigration relief (1 year) to potential witnesses who are victims of severe forms of trafficking	Enables victims of human trafficking to live and work in the U.S. for four years
Provides work authorization and access to refugee benefits	Allows application for adjustment into lawful permanent resident status after three years with T visa or after conclusion of criminal trafficking cases
	Permits petition for victim's spouses and children (or parents and unmarried siblings under 18 if the victim is under 21)
	Number of visas is capped at 5,000 annually

United States Department of Health and Human Services

The key to eligibility, however, is the assistance in the investigation and prosecution of the accused trafficker. The exception to this rule is if the victim is under the age of eighteen, which makes the victim automatically eligible for immigration assistance with or without prosecutorial assistance.

The identification and protection of victims is crucial in the battle against human trafficking. However, there are other issues at play that make complete eradication virtually impossible. These issues are considered to be the real causes of trafficking, which can easily be summed up in two categories: the vulnerable status of migrating groups, and the demand for the commodities proffered at prices made available through slave labor.

Vulnerable Status

As discussed throughout the chapters of this book, some of the factors associated with human trafficking include "an increase in poverty and unemployment...the lack of educational and economic opportunities...the rise of globalization and increased mobility, the expansion of transnational organized crime, [and] the widening economic gap between developing and developed countries" (Yen, 2008: 657). These matters are further affected by ethnic, religious, gender, or age discrimination, making certain segments of the population more vulnerable to human trafficking, including women, children, and members of indigenous minority groups.

Aside from the issues indicative of the origin countries, destination countries, such as the United States, may maintain policies that contribute to the emergence of a population more vulnerable to human trafficking. Such policies may those relating to immigration. As the United States tightens immigration policies, with a greater reliance on border control as an effort of national security as well as a trafficking reduction strategy, the reality is that "restrictive immigration policies and border controls could...be seen to be increasing the likelihood that would-be migrants will be trafficked and also mean that those who have been trafficked are likely to be returned to their countries of origin, exposing them to the same conditions which persuaded them to migrate in the first place" (Freedman 2003: 119–120). Thus, efforts to reduce trafficking are actually increasing the risk of trafficking in the United States.

It is clear that certain populations are more vulnerable to becoming victims of human trafficking than others. In addition, some immigration policies promote trafficking rather than reduce it. And yet, the demand for the services provided through slave labor is truly what pushes the trafficking industry. While the demand exists, traffickers will continue to prey on vulnerable populations with promises of opportunity and economic freedom.

Demand

Modern-day slavery benefits consumers and companies alike, and that is the most basic explanation as to why slavery persists despite its unconstitutionality. First of all, U.S. companies reap huge profits by selling cheap goods made with slave labor. Whether it is clothing, produce, gems, or chocolate, companies are able to make tremendous profits through the use of slave labor. For example, the tomato industry is highly profitable in that workers are averaging $50 for every two tons of tomatoes harvested (less than a penny per pound). At the same time, companies are selling tomatoes at an average of $2.00–$3.00 per pound depending on the season and location. Focusing on the low end of the estimate, it is clear that the cost of tomato increases by over 200 percent from the harvest to the grocery store shelf. Of course, farmers will argue that the markup represents the cost of transportation and production, but this does not fully explain the substantial disparity between the salary of the migrant worker and the cost of the product. More importantly, as prices are inflated in various sectors throughout the country, the price of produce also increases, creating a markup of prices that will not disrupt profits. To put it bluntly, the tomato industry in Florida alone is a multi-million-dollar industry—a profit made possible through the victimization of thousands of migrant workers.

Aside from the company profits that are being made, the consumer must also be considered, for U.S. consumers are able enjoy cheap goods made with slave labor. Unfortunately, our consumerist society is so influenced by finding the lowest prices that avoiding products produced with slave labor is virtually impossible. Many readers may already be aware of the conditions of work associated with the products that they consume, yet at the same time, the organizational structure of society makes it so that we all encourage slave labor one way or another. Generally speaking, in a time of economic crisis, most citizens do not want to pay more for what they already cannot afford. Therefore, we buy the products, somewhat aware that the only way a deal is possible is through the exploitation of a member of a vulnerable community, yet our individualistic nature overshadows the moral issue at hand. And so, most of us buy and consume without question as a way to possibly ease our own concerns.

The purchasing of cheap goods produced through slave labor is not entirely the fault of the consumer, for we are all living within a state structure that has historically supported slavery in all forms. Until those invisible lines are exposed, and the true benefactors of our consumerism are identified as facilitators of slavery, the cycle will continue. The inability to properly prosecute the key offenders has led to the permanence of slavery in our society. Because we as consumers cannot escape the structure, let alone expose the benefactors, we are left with very few options when trying to live a "slave-free" life. In other words, we may make attempts to buy slave-free items, but the reality is that products produced through the exploitation and oppression of vulnerable groups are so rooted in the institutional structure that to completely remove ourselves from this capitalist system that supports slavery is virtually impossible. Therefore, we must continue to educate ourselves and to protest those industries that blatantly utilize slave labor to produce cheap goods without any effort to improve the pay or work conditions for their laborers.

Companies and consumers are not the only benefactors of slave labor. Thousands of American families benefit from the cooking, cleaning, child rearing, and work of domestic servants. This is especially true in those cases where a young child is bought as a sex slave with a secondary occupational front of domestic servant or nanny. These children provide domestic services to families for little to no pay, with minimal living quarters (e.g., closets, basements) and no personal space or freedom. The families that benefit from these children may either be completely aware of the enslavement with no moral concern for the exploitation of these children, or they may have fooled themselves into believing that they are assisting these children who "have no other options." This latter ruse is encouraged through newspaper classifieds that advertise the work of a nanny or domestic servant in return for living quarters and food. There is no mention of pay, and therefore, the families that take in these children as domestic laborers feel that the pay for their services should be no more than in the form of food and living space. Despite the lack of payment and substandard living situation, many of these families employing domestic assistance believe that they are providing a better life to the children, rather than exploiting their labor. This neutralization technique is common for this form of human trafficking, especially when the child has multiple tasks, including services that are sexual in nature. This trafficking overlap leads to the final benefactors of slave labor, which are the American men who purchase the sexual services of women forced into the sex industry.

As noted in Chapter 3, thousands of American men purchase sexual services from women and children throughout the country. Some of these men may actually purchase the child to keep enslaved the home as a personal sex object, and may choose to pass the child around to friends deemed worthy of such services. Other men go to prostitutes who are controlled by traffickers and/or pimps, while many men may choose to travel to brothels to purchase sexual services. Lastly, men may purchase the sexual services of women who have been trafficked into the adult entertainment industry, and although this may or may not include sexual intercourse, the women who are trafficked into this industry are as controlled, victimized, and exploited as their counterparts in the prostitution industry. Men who purchase women and children for their sexual services are not in search of companionship; rather they are seeking relationships with no ties, while at the same time fulfilling nonconsensual violent and pedophilic fantasies that would be taboo in a traditional consensual sexual relationship. Commodified sex is easily accessible because of trafficking, and therefore has been a major component in the demand for modern-day slavery.

Taken together, there is virtually no individual in the United States who does not benefit from slave labor in one way or another. Whether it is for a profit, the purchase of a cheap good, domestic assistance, or a sexual service, we are all guilty of fostering modern-day slavery in one form or another in the United States. This facilitation is furthered by justifications based on anti-immigrant sentiments. Although it can easily be said that not every American has strong stances against immigration, the voting citizens, politicians, and media mouths that do speak out against immigration, while proposing various immigration policies, create a great obstacle for those attempting to educate others to the horrors associated with human trafficking. To argue "If you don't like it, go home," or "They shouldn't complain, because they are here illegally" does not solve the trafficking problem. In reality, the anti-immigrant attitude criminalizes victims and promotes future trafficking. Furthermore, the demand is augmented by our own demand, for as previously stated, the majority of us are in need of the products and services yielded by the undocumented individuals trafficked into the United States. Therefore, rather than blaming undocumented immigrants for their own victimization, we need to look beyond the surface and evaluate the demand for human trafficking and our own contribution to modern-day slavery. Only then can we take the steps needed to begin improving the living and work conditions of undocumented immigrants, while preventing the future victimization of the thousands of women, men, and children trafficked into the United States.

Immokalee in Context

In virtually every community in the United States, slavery exists, and it exists in all forms, from sexual servitude to panhandling. The victims of trafficking in Immokalee are unique in their individual experiences, but the practice of modern-day slavery is in and of itself not exclusive to the small town in the backlands of the southern Florida landscape. Rather, it exists in border towns, in the Midwest, in large cities, and in small agricultural communities. Members of the migrant and undocumented class are victimized and exploited throughout the country. Domestic citizens are sold by their parents to support a drug habit, or children run away and become vulnerable to preying pimps looking for the next vulnerable target. I found Immokalee to be an exceptional case study, but everyone who reads from this book can learn from this example.

As discussed earlier, victim identification is the first step to reducing human trafficking, and identification may only be improved through adequate training. However, advocates and local police across the country have taken steps beyond identification to assist victims and eradicate trafficking in their own community. For example, in North Carolina, where slavery has been identified in the tobacco fields, the Farmworking Unit of Legal Aid of North Carolina (LANC) has advocates who go out to the fields weekly to educate farmworkers regarding their legal rights, as well as to provide information for immigration assistance. This not only serves to identify victims of trafficking, but also provides an outlet for victims who wish to report their slavery. Because of their legal advocacy role , members of the LANC may also provide assistance if the victim chooses to aid in the prosecution of the trafficker.

In addition to LANC, advocacy-based groups such as the Farm Advocacy Network (FAN) of North Carolina, collaborate to "to bring workers' voices to the legislative process" (www.ncfan.org, accessed July 2011). Some legislative amendments for which FAN has advocated are better workplace laws to improve the life and well-being not only of tobacco farmers, but also of poultry farmers. Since its inception in 2003, FAN has "[improved] farmworker housing conditions across the state by securing passage of amendments to the North Carolina Migrant Housing Act; [supported] legislation that would reduce the risk of pesticide exposure and ensure that employers take precautions to keep workers safe; [and participated] in vital research projects about the on-the-job dangers to worker health and safety in the agricultural and poultry industries" (ibid). Just as in Immokalee, legal professionals and nongovernmental advocates are taking measures to protect the workers in the state of North Carolina, while at the same time pressuring the state government to improve work conditions and eradicate slavery in the agricultural sector.

In the Midwest, St. Louis police are working with local nongovernmental groups to identify sex trafficking in the city. Specifically, local police work with the International Institute, a group that "[works] with law enforcement to rescue individuals in [human trafficking] situations and ensure safety for those rescued…[while providing] whatever victim services are needed, including housing, clothing, food and other basic necessities" (www.iistl.org, accessed May 2011). Additionally, the International Institute provides counseling services and immigration legal support (ibid). The local police in St.

Louis not only work with the International Institute but also network with an entire human trafficking joint working group, which includes members from Catholic Charities, the Department of Homeland Security, the Department of Labor, the FBI, the U.S. Attorney's Office, and researchers from Washington University. The collaborative efforts of the working group have proven to be successful in that more and more sex-related crimes are being identified as potential trafficking cases, thereby illustrating the reality of sex trafficking in the St. Louis area. Identified cases from St. Louis include a Craigslist interstate prostitution scam, exposure of which resulted in the perpetrator receiving five years in prison, and a 2009 trafficking case in which the trafficker received twenty years in federal prison for forcing a young child into prostitution (Department of Justice, 2009).[3] Again, it was the networking efforts between local and federal law enforcement with nongovernmental advocates that assisted in the successful efforts toward the eradication of trafficking in the St. Louis area.

Such efforts in these communities not only provide the reader with additional examples of human trafficking in the United States, but also emphasize the steps that are being taken to reduce local trafficking activities while protecting the victims. The United States is a hot-spot destination for human trafficking, and readers need to be aware of the indicators, as well as what efforts have proven to be successful in protecting victims and punishing the offenders, including training and awareness that trafficking is occurring in our own communities. A key lesson that can be taken away from the Immokalee example is the importance of collaborative networking between nongovernmental advocates and legal professionals at the county, state, and federal levels. Every successfully prosecuted case identified in this book was the result of the proper training of local law enforcement, and the assistance of advocates working for nongovernmental organizations. Rather than creating a divide due to conflicting missions, members and NGOs and law enforcement working together become an effective front against human trafficking. Modern-day slavery is in our back yard, in virtually every American community. Slavery in Immokalee is not occurring in a vacuum, and, realizing this, readers may take the efforts that are being made in this small community as a lesson of awareness and a call to action to identify and protect victims of human trafficking in their own communities.

Concluding Thoughts

The economic and structural foundation of the United States has historically been built and maintained through systems of slavery. Although legally abolished with the writing of the Thirteenth Amendment to the Constitution of the United States, slavery has continued to exist in various forms, including debt bondage, forced labor, domestic servitude, and peonage. This book has been my attempt not only to expose modern-day slavery in its various forms, but also to highlight one small community in southern Florida that has made great strides in attempting to improve the lives of the thousands of migrant workers and their families that are trafficked to the small town every harvest season.

Because farms in Immokalee, Florida, produce the majority of tomatoes in the United States, the town is a prime destination for migrant workers vulnerable to human trafficking. The tomato industry is one of the last agricultural sectors to rely on humans, rather than machinery, to pick the produce. Therefore, cheap migrant work is valuable to the farmers, who for the most part have turned a blind eye to the slavery evident in the fields. At the same time, Immokalee is also secluded from the neighboring wealthy communities, which allows for the sexual victimization of women and children with little notice from the prying eyes of moral crusaders. The sexual exploitation in Immokalee is furthered by the presence on the edge of town of the Seminole casino, which attracts tourists and residents alike to purchase sexual services. However, tourists, as discussed earlier in the book, are more likely to purchase the actual individual for their own personal sex object, whereas migrant laborers are more likely to use the services offered in the brothels and "bars."

Despite the fact that Immokalee exists as a microcosm of the larger issue of human trafficking evident throughout the United States, community and legal advocates are proactive in identifying and protecting victims while at the same time punishing offenders. It is this advocacy that makes Immokalee exceptional, for the attempts that are made and the victories that are won are constantly obstructed by immigration enforcement responsibilities, cuts in funding, and recommended policy changes. Yet, the struggle endures, and the belief among these actors remains that to pull one person out of the system of slavery is an achievement like no other. And although there are many more individuals that need to be protected from the cycle of slavery, each day offers a new opportunity to identify and protect another person. For those who remain unidentified, local law enforcement officers attempt to maintain a sense of community built on trust, communication, and education.

From the first time I was shocked by the cultural and economic contrast between Immokalee and the neighboring communities of southern Florida to the last time I drove down the main street out of town, I have truly been impacted by the individuals I have met and the stories I have heard. Each voice remains with me, and it is my expectation that the stories hidden throughout the vast terrain of southern Florida will finally be told. Each day, the citizens of Immokalee have new obstacles to overcome, and what tomorrow brings remains unknown. What is known is that within a structure of horror and tragedy, hope has emerged. Although I take the pessimistic belief that slavery will never be eradicated, I also truly believe that for the victims of trafficking in Immokalee Florida, hope for a better tomorrow does exist. I also believe that through the valiant efforts of community and legal advocates alike, hope is possible today, as will it remain to be tomorrow.

---

[1] In November, 2010, the demotion of the chief assistant attorney was the only management change made by O'Neill.

[2] Information derived from acf.hhs.gov/trafficking/about/cert_victims.html

[3] Information provided by a St. Louis Police Department Detective.

Appendix A

Trafficking in Persons by Country (Tier Ranking)

(1 = Tier One; 2 = Tier Two; 2WL = Tier Two Watch List; 3 = Third Tier)

Afghanistan	2WL	Greece	2	Oman	2
Albania	2	Guatemala	2WL	Pakistan	2
Algeria	2WL	Guinea	2WL	Palau	2
Angola	2	Guinea-Bissau	2WL	Panama	2WL
Antigua & Barbuda	2	Guyana	2WL	Papua New Guinea	3
Argentina	2	Honduras	2	Paraguay	2
Armenia	2	Hong Kong	2	Peru	2
Australia	1	Hungary	2	Philippines	2WL
Austria	1	Iceland	2	Poland	1
Azerbaijan	2WL	India	2WL	Portugal	2
The Bahamas	2	Indonesia	2	Qatar	2WL
Bahrain	2	Iran	3	Romania	2
Bangladesh	2WL	Iraq	2WL	Russia	2WL
Barbados	2WL	Ireland	1	Rwanda	2
Belarus	2	Israel	2	St. Vincent & the Grenadines	2WL

Belgium	1	Italy	1	Saudi Arabia	3
Belize	2WL	Jamaica	2	Senegal	2WL
Benin	2	Japan	2	Serbia	2
Bolivia	2	Jordan	2	Sierra Leone	2
Bosnia & Herzegovina	1	Kazakhstan	2WL	Singapore	2WL
Botswana	2	Kenya	2	Slovak Republic	2
Brazil	2	Kiribati	2WL	Slovenia	1
Brunei	2WL	Korea, North	3	South Africa	2
Bulgaria	2	Korea, South	1	Spain	1
Burkina Faso	2	Kosovo	2	Sri Lanka	2WL
Burma	3	Kuwait	3	Sudan	3
Burundi	2	Kyrgyz Republic	2	Suriname	2
Cambodia	2	Laos	2WL	Swaziland	2WL
Cameroon	2WL	Latvia	2	Sweden	1
Canada	1	Lebanon	2WL	Switzerland	2
Central African Rep.	2WL	Lesotho	2WL	Syria	2WL
Chad	2WL	Liberia	2	Taiwan	1
Chile	2	Libya	2WL	Tajikistan	2WL
China (PRC)	2WL	Lithuania	1	Tanzania	2WL
Colombia	1	Luxembourg	1	Thailand	2WL

Congo (DRC)	3	Macau	2	Timor-Leste	2
Congo (ROC)	2WL	Macedonia	2	Togo	2
Costa Rica	2	Madagascar	2WL	Trinidad & Tobago	2WL
Cote d'Ivoire	2WL	Malawi	2	Tunisia	2WL
Croatia	1	Malaysia	2WL	Turkey	2
Cuba	3	Maldives	2WL	Turkmenistan	2WL
Cyprus	2	Mali	2WL	Uganda	2
Czech Republic	1	Malta	2WL	Ukraine	2
Denmark	1	Mauritania	3	United Arab Emirates	2
Djibouti	2	Mauritius	1	United Kingdom	1
Dominican Republic	3	Mexico	2	United States of America	1
Ecuador	2	Micronesia	2WL	Uruguay	2
Egypt	2	Moldova	2WL	Uzbekistan	2WL
El Salvador	2	Mongolia	2	Venezuela	2WL
Equatorial Guinea	2WL	Montenegro	2	Vietnam	2WL
Eritrea	3	Morocco	2	Yemen	2WL
Estonia	2	Mozambique	2WL	Zambia	2
Ethiopia	2	Namibia	2	Zimbabwe	3
Fiji	2WL	Nepal	2	Haiti	SC
Finland	1	Netherlands	1	Somalia	SC

France	1	Neth. Antilles	2		
Gabon	2WL	New Zealand	1		
The Gambia	2	Nicaragua	2WL		
Georgia	1	Niger	2WL		
Germany	1	Nigeria	1		
Ghana	2	Norway	1		

data derived from www.state.gov, accessed 2011

Appendix B

Local Law Enforcement Outreach Brochure: English Version (also available in Spanish)

Human Trafficking Indicators

General Indicators
- Live on or near work premises
- Restricted or controlled communication or transportation
- Frequently moved by traffickers
- Large number of occupants for living space
- Lack of private space or personal possessions
- Limited knowledge of how to get around in a community

Physical Indicators
- Injuries from beatings or weapons
- Signs of torture (e.g., cigarette burns)
- Brands or scarring indicating ownership
- Signs of malnourishment

Financial/Legal Indicators
- Someone else has possession of legal or travel documents
- Lack of financial records
- Existing debt issues
- One attorney claiming to represent multiple illegal aliens detained at different locations
- Third party who insists on interpreting

Labor Camp Sweatshop Indicators
- Security intended to keep victims confined
- Barbed wire or bars on windows
- Self-contained camps
- Bouncers, guards or guard dogs

Brothel Indicators
- Large amounts of cash and condoms
- Customer logbook or receipt book
- Sparse rooms
- Men come and go frequently

If you suspect someone is a victim of human trafficking call:

Collier County Sheriff's Office
Victims Advocate Unit
239.793.9176
after hours:
239.793.9300

Collier County Coalition Against
Human Trafficking
www.ccaht.org

U.S. Department of Justice
Trafficking Information and Referral Hotline
at 1.888.373.7888

Naples Police and Emergency Services
239.213.4844

Marco Island Police Department
239.389.5050

Coalition of Immokalee Workers
239.657.8311

www.colliersheriff.org

In an EMERGENCY call 9-1-1

Informational human trafficking websites:
www.humantrafficking.org
www.childtrafficking.com
www.antislavery.org
www.floridafreedom.org
www.cahr.fsu.edu
www.cew-online.org

The project was supported by Award No. 2005-VT-BX-002, awarded by the Department of Justice, Office of Justice Programs, Bureau of Justice Assistance. The opinions, findings, and conclusions or recommendations expressed in this publication/program/exhibition are those of the author(s) and do not necessarily reflect the views of the Department of Justice.

Human
Trafficking

**Breaking the Chains
of Slavery in Collier County**

Collier County Sheriff's Office
Human Trafficking Unit
3301 Tamiami Trail East, Bldg. J
Naples, Florida 34112-4902
239.793.9176
victimsrv@colliersheriff.net

Sheriff Kevin Rambosk

Bibliography

Antislavery International (2011) www.antislavery.org.

Arizona Senate Bill 1070 www.azleg.gov/legtext/49leg/2r/bills/sb1070s.pdf

Arnold, C. (2007) "Racial Profiling in Immigration Enforcement: State and Local Agreements to Enforce Federal Immigration Law." *Arizona Law Review,* Vol. 49: 113–142.

Asanok et al. v. Million Express Manpower, Inc. et al. (2007) North Carolina Eastern District Office, Case No. 5:2007cv00048.

Belser, P. (2005) "Forced Labor and Human Trafficking: Estimating the Profits." International
Labour Organization, seattleagainstslavery.org.

Bhabha, J. (2003) "More Than Their Share of Sorrows." *St. Louis University Public Law Review* Vol. 253.

Bowe, J. (2007) *Nobodies: Modern American Slave Labor and the Dark Side of the New Global Economy.* Random House, New York.

Brass, T. (1999) *Towards a Political Economy of Unfree Labour: Case Studies and Debates* Frank Cass, Portland, OR.

California Alliance to Combat Trafficking and Slavery Task Force (2007) "Human Trafficking in California" http://ag.ca.gov/publications/Human_Trafficking_Final_Report.pdf.

Capps, R. (2009) "Local Enforcement of Immigration Laws: Evolution of the 287(g) Program and its Potential Impacts on Local Communities." In *The Role of Local Police: Striking a Balance Between Immigration Enforcement and Civil Liberties,* the Police Foundation of Washington, D.C., April.

Chapkis, W. (2003) "Trafficking, Migration, and the Law: Protecting Innocents, Punishing Immigrants." *Gender and Society* 17 (6): 923–937.

Cholewinski, R. (1997) *Migrant Workers in International Human Rights Law: Their Protection in Countries of Employment.* Oxford University Press, New York.

Civil Society www.civilsocietyhelps.org

Clawson, H., M. Layne, and K. Small (2006) "Estimating Human Trafficking Into the United States: Development of a Methodology" http://www.ncjrs.gov/pdffiles1/nij/grants/215475.pdf

Coalition of Immokalee Workers, www.ciw-online.org

Coalition of Immokalee Workers (2007) *Facts and Figures of Farmworkers,* www.ciw-online.org/images/Facts_and_Figures_07.pdf.

Cornwell, B. (2009) "Immokalee: Where Fact and Legend Collide." *Fort Myers* [Florida] *Weekly,* May 6.

Davis, R. C., and E. Erez (1998) "Immigrant Populations as Victims: Toward a

Multicultural Criminal Justice System." National Institute of Justice. www.nij.gov

Davis, R. C., E. Erez, and N. Avitabile (2001) "Access to Justice for Immigrants Who Are Victimized: The Perspectives of Police and Prosecutors" *Criminal Justice Policy Review* 12 (3): 183–196.

Davis, R. C., and N. Henderson (2003) "Willingness to Report Crimes: The Role of Ethnic Group Membership and Community Efficacy." *Crime and Delinquency* 49 (4): 564–580.

Decker, S. H., P. G. Lewis, D. M. Provine, and M. W. Varsanyi (2009) "On the Frontier of Local Law Enforcement: Local Police and Federal Immigration Law." In *Immigration, Crime, and Justice*, ed. W. F. McDonald. Emerald Group, UK.

Dinan, S., and K. Rowland (2010) "Justice: Sanctuary Cities Safe from Law." *The Washington Times,* July 14.

Domhoff, G. W. (1990) *The Power Elite and the State: How Policy Is Made in America.* Walter de Gruyter, New York.

Engerman, S. L. (1986) "Servants to Slaves to Servants: Contract Labour and European Expansion." In *Colonialism and Migration: Indentured Labour Before and After Slavery,* ed. P. C. Emmer. Martinus Nijhoff, Boston.

Estabrook, B. (2009, March) "Politics of the Place: The Price of Tomatoes" *Gourmet* magazine, www.gourmet.com.

——— (2011) *Tomatoland: How Modern Industrial Agriculture Destroyed Our Most Alluring Fruit.* Andrew McMeels, Kansas City, MO.

Farmworker Advocacy Network (2011) www.ncfan.org

Farrell, A. (2009) "State and Local Law Enforcement Responses to Human Trafficking: Why So Few Trafficking Cases Are Identified in the United States." In *Immigration, Crime and Justice*, ed. W. F. McDonald. Emerald Group, Bingley, UK.

Farrell, A., J. McDevitt, S. Fahy (2007) "Understanding and Improving Law Enforcement Responses to Human Trafficking." U.S. Department of Justice. www.justice.gov.

Feingold, D. A. (2005) "Think Again Human Trafficking" www.preventhumantrafficking.org.

Fleck, F. (2004) "Children Are Main Victims of Trafficking." *British Medical Journal* 328 (7447): 1036.

Florida Modern-Day Slavery Museum (2010) http://www.ciw-online.org/freedom_march/MuseumBookletWeb.pdf

Free the Slaves (accessed 2010) www.freetheslaves.net.

Freedman, J. (2003) "Selling Sex: Trafficking, Prostitution, and Sex Work among Migrant Women in Europe." in *Gender and Insecurity,* ed. J. Freedman. Ashgate, Burlington, VT.

Frost, C. (2008) "Statement before the Senate Health, Education, Labor, and Pensions Committee," April 15. Retrieved from help.senate.gov.

Gillespie, P. (2010) "New US Attorney Demotes Chief of Fort Myers Office" *The News Press- Ft. Myers, FL,* November 19

Haynes, D. (2006) "Client Centered Human Rights Advocacy" *Clinical Law Review,* Fall

Heil, E. C. (2008) "Powerless Resistance: A Theoretical Discussion of Power, Resistance, and the Brazilian Landless Movement." ProQuest Dissertations & Theses (PQDT) Database.

Higbie, F. T. (2003) *Indispensible Outcasts: Hobo Workers and Community in the American Midwest, 1880-1930*. University of Illinois Press, Chicago.

Holt-Giménez, E. (2009) "The Coalition of Immokalee Workers: Fighting Modern Day Slavery in the Industrial Food System" foodfirst.org

Heuvel, K.V. (2010) "Florida's Modern Slavery...The Museum." *The Nation,* March 29.

Hughes, D.M. (2005) "The Demand for Victims of Sex Trafficking" http://www.uri.edu/artsci/wms/hughes/demand_for_victims.pdf

Human Trafficking Awareness www.humantraffickingawareness.org

International Institute (2011) www.iistl.org

International Labour Organization (2009) www.ilo.org

Joshi, A. (2002) "The Face of Human Trafficking." *Hastings Women's Law Journal* 13 (1): 18–40.

Kangaspunta, K. (2010) "A Short History of Trafficking in Persons," *Freedom From Fear* magazine, www.freedomfromfearmagazine.org.

Khashu, A. (2009) "The Role of Local Police: Striking a Balance Between Immigration Enforcement and Civil Liberties." The Police Foundation of Washington D.C., April. http://policefoundation.org/strikingabalance/strikingabalance.html

Kittrie, O. F. (2006) "Federalism, Deportation and Crime Victims Afraid to Call the Police." *Iowa Law Review* 91: 1449–1508.

Kloer, A. (2010) "Slave Labor on Hawaii's Second Largest Farm," change.org, January 15.

Kyle, D., and M. Scarcelli (2009) "Migrant Smuggling and the Violence Question: Evolving Illicit Migration Markets for Cuban and Haitian Refugees." *Crime Law and Social Change* 52: 297-311

Legal Aid of North Carolina (2010) www.farmworkerlanc.org.

Lendman, S. (2009) "Modern Slavery in America." *Global Research,* March 6.

Martínez and Valenzuela (2006) "Immigration and Crime: Race, Ethnicity, and Violence" New York University Press, New York

Maxwell, B. (2009) "Gov. Crist Backs Farmworkers." *St. Petersburg Times,* April 5, www.tampabay.com.

Meissner, D., and D. Kerwin (2009) "DHS and Immigration: Taking Stock and Correcting Course." Migration Policy Institute, http://www.migrationpolicy.org/pubs/DHS_Feb09.pdf.

Miller, M. (2002) "Immigration Law: Assessing New Immigration Enforcement Strategies and the Criminalization of Migration." *Emory Law Journal* 51 (3): 963–976.

Montgomery, D. (1993) *Citizen Worker: The Experience of Workers in the United States with Democracy and the Free Market during the Nineteenth Century.* Cambridge University Press, New York.

Mutua, M. (2001) "Savages, Victims, and the Saviors: The Metaphor of Human Rights." *Harvard International Law Journal*, vol. 201.

National Center for Farmworkers Health, Inc. (2009) "Migrant and Seasonal Farmworkers Demographics" www.ncfh.org

Olivas, M. (2007) "Immigration Related State Statutes and Local Ordinances: Preemption, Prejudice, and the Proper Role for Enforcement." *University of Chicago Legal Forum* 27: 27–56.

Parra-Chico, M. F. (2008). "An Up-Close Perspective: The Enforcement of Federal Immigration Laws by State and Local Police." *Seattle Journal for Social Justice* 7 (1).

Perez, E. (2010) "Major Grower to Join Wage Plan." *The Wall Street Journal,* October 13, online.wsj.com.

Pham, H. (2008) "Problems Facing the First Generation of Immigration Laws." *Hofstra Law Review* 36 (4).

Plyler v. Doe, 457 U.S.202 (1982).

Raymond, J. G., and D. M. Hughes (2001) "Sex Trafficking of Women in the United States: International and Domestic Trends." Submitted to the Department of Justice, Document Number: 187774, April 17 https://www.ncjrs.gov/pdffiles1/nij/grants/187774.pdf

Rijken, C., and D. Koster (2008) "A Human Rights Based Approach to Trafficking in Human Beings in Theory and Practice." *Social Science Research Network.* papers.ssrn.com/sol3/papers.cfm?abstract_id=1135108

Rosario, R. (2006) "Human Trafficking Plagues Even Minnesota – Midwest U.S." http://www.wunrn.com/news/2006/03_26_06/033106_trafficking_midwest.htm.

Sanctuary Cities Information Website www.sanctuarycities.info

Schlosser, E. (2007) "Penny Foolish." *New York Times,* November 29.

Seghetti, L. M., K. Ester, and M. J. Garcia (2009) "Enforcing Immigration Law: The Role of State and Local Law Enforcement." Washington D.C., Congressional Research Service.

Sessions, J., and C. Hayden (2005) "Globalization, Security, and Human Rights: Immigration in the Twenty-First Century." *Stanford Law and Policy Review* Vol. 323.

Skogan, W. (2009) "Policing Immigrant Communities in the United States." In *Immigration, Crime, and Justice.* ed. William F. McDonald. Emerald Group, UK.

Southern Poverty Law Center (2009) "Intelligence Report about Hate Crimes," http://www.splcenter.org/.

Taylor, I., and R. Jamieson (1999) "Sex Trafficking and the Mainstream of Market Culture." *Crime, Law, and Social Change* 32 (3): 257–278.

Tiefenbrun, S. (2002) "The Saga of Susannah – A U.S. Remedy for Sex Trafficking in Women: The Victims of Trafficking and Violence Protection Act of 2000." *Utah Law Review* 107: 107–175.

Trafficking of Victims Protection Act (Victims of Trafficking and Violence Protection Act) P.L. 106–386, Oct. 28, 2000.

Trafficking Victims Protection Reauthorization Act (2008) H. R. 7311.

Tuirán, R. (accessed 2011) "Past and Present of the Mexican Immigration to the United States" Farmworkers.org.

Turner, J., and L. Kelly (2009) "Trade Secrets: Intersections between Diasporas and Crime Groups in the Constitution of the Human Trafficking Chain." *British Journal of Criminology* 49 (2): 184–201.

UNDOC (United Nations Office on Drugs and Crime). "Human Trafficking," http://www.unodc.org/unodc/en/human-trafficking/what-is-human-trafficking.html.

United Nations (2000) "Protocol to Prevent, Suppress, and Punish Trafficking in Persons, Especially Women and Children, Supplementing the United Nations Convention against Transnational Crime," www.uncjin.org.

———— (2009) "Trafficking in Persons: Analysis on Europe." United Nations Office on Drugs and Crime, Vienna.

University of California, Berkeley (2004) "Hidden Slaves: Forced Labor in the United States." Free the Slaves and Human Rights Center, Berkeley, CA

United Nations (2009) "Global Report on Trafficking in Persons." United Nations Office on Drugs and Crimes.

United States Citizen and Immigration Services (2011) www.uscis.gov

United States Department of Health and Human Services (2011) http://www.acf.hhs.gov/trafficking/about/cert_victims.html

United States Department of Homeland Security, Illinois (2010) "Human Trafficking in Illinois" www.dhs.state.il.us.

United States Department of Justice (2002). Press Release PR# 038, January 24.

———— (2008)"Immokalee, Florida, Family Charged with Forcing Immigrants Into Forced Labor," January 17.

———— (2008) "Brothers Plead Guilty to Enslaving Farmworkers in Florida, Co-Defendants Plead Guilty to Related Felonies," September 3

United States Department of Labor (2004) "The National Agricultural Workers Survey,"www.doleta.gov.

United States Department of State (2009) "Trafficking in Persons Report," www.state.gov/g/tip/rls/tiprpt/2010.

————(2010) "Trafficking in Persons Report," www.state.gov/g/tip/rls/tiprpt/2010.

United States Immigration Customs and Enforcement (2010) www.ice.gov

United States vs. Cuello (1999)

United States vs. Tecum (2001) 01-10822-JJ

Unknown Author (2007) "Modern-Day Slavery: Human-trafficking Investigation Leads to 16 Johnson County Raids." *Kansas City Star,* May 11.

———— (2008) "Massage Parlor Owner/Operators Plead Guilty To Human Trafficking." *Kansas City Business Journal.*

———— (2009) "Naval Recruiter Accused of Child Sex Trafficking." KNBC, www.knbc.com

———— (2009) "Couple Given Stiffer Penalties for Hiding Pinay Maid for 19 Years," abs-cbnNEWS.com, June 10.

———— (2011) "New Charges Filed against Kirkwood Man in Sex-slave Case," www.stltoday.com, March 31.

Vaughan, J. M., and J. R. Edwards (2009) "The 287(g) Program: Protecting Home Towns and Homeland." Center for Immigration Studies, October.

Weissman, D. M., R. C. Headen, and K. L. Parker (2009) "The Policy and Politics of Local Immigration Enforcement Laws: 287(g) Program in North Carolina." American Civil Liberties Union and Immigration and Human Rights Policy Clinic, North Carolina, February, http://acluofnc.org/files/287gexecutivesummary_0.pdf.

Wheeler, K., W. Zhao, K. Kelleher, L. Stallones, and H. Xiang (2010) "Immigrants as Crime Victims: Experiences of Personal Nonfatal Victimization." *American Journal of Industrial Medicine* 53 (4): 435–442.

Williams, A. (2010) "Immokalee Slavery Story Topic of Day on Global Radio," www.news-press.com.

Wilson, D. G., W. F. Walsh, S. Kleuber (2006) "Trafficking in Human Beings: Training and Services among US Law Enforcement Agencies." *Police Practice and Research* 7 (2): 149–160.

Wilson, J. M., and E. Dalton (2008) "Human Trafficking in the Heartland: Variation in Law Enforcement." *Journal of Contemporary Criminal Justice* 24 (3) 296–313.

Wing, N. (2010) "Rick Scott Endorses Arizona-Style Immigration Enforcement." *Huffington Post*, December 2, www.huffingtonpost.com

www.humantrafficking.org (2010).

Yen, I. (2008) "Of Vice and Men: A New Approach to Eradicating Sex Trafficking By Reducing Male Demand through Educational Programs and Abolitionist Legislation." *The Journal of Criminal Law & Criminology* 98 (2): 653–686.

Yu Perkins, W. (2005) "Vital Voices: Advocacy and Service Work of NGOs in the Fight against Human Trafficking." *UN Chronicle,* vol. 1.

Zinn, H. (1995) *A People's History of the United States: 1492–Present.* Harper Collins Publishers, New York.

Zonta International www.zonta.org.

Index

abuse, physical 26, 36, 38
advocacy groups 22, 34, 58, 90, 117-18, 129
Africans, enslaved 27
agricultural communities 6, 48, 126, 146
agricultural sector 13, 47, 60, 147, 149
Agricultural Slave 22, 26, 37, 48-9
  identified 49
anti-immigrant sentiments 46, 81, 146
anti-trafficking advocates 122
anti-trafficking efforts 4, 13, 20, 24, 78, 122
anti-trafficking initiatives 122
anti-trafficking movement 114
Arizona 96, 135, 138
Arizona-style immigration enforcement policy in Florida 135, 136
arrests 20, 22, 73, 86, 89, 95-6
assistant US attorney, chief 136
assistant US district attorney 23, 53-4, 98, 101-4, 112, 121-2, 127, 130
authorities, federal 83, 124-5

bars 6-7, 65, 97, 128, 149
beatings 39, 41, 44, 49
bondage 31, 44, 58
  trafficked 100
border control 17, 46, 143
brothels 8, 15, 54, 60, 62-7, 70-1, 74-5, 77, 98, 101, 129-30, 139, 145, 149
  working 56, 63, 65
buyers 58, 61-72, 74-5
  independent 62, 66-8, 70-1
  private 62, 77

California 14-16, 19, 48

California Alliance to Combat Trafficking and Slavery Task Force 15
campaign 111, 123, 125-6, 128, 134
  anti-slavery 123
Catholic Charities 21-2, 24, 112, 118, 120-2, 126, 148
Chandler Roundup 88
child victims 59
chilling effect 86, 90-1, 95, 100, 108, 137
cities, sanctuary 138-9
CIW (Coalition of Immokalee Workers) 6, 8, 22-4, 34, 36-7, 40, 48-50, 99, 100, 103, 111-12, 118, 123-8, 130-2, 134-5, 139
CIW headquarters 40, 99-100
Coalition leaders 123
Coalition of Immokalee Workers see CIW
Collier County 23, 80, 83, 85, 93, 95, 99, 136-37
Collier County Division of Human Trafficking 21, 80, 98-9
Collier County Sheriff 21, 91, 112
commercial sexual exploitation 11-13, 16, 23, 55, 57, 98
community
  farming 50
  illegal 23
  laboring 15
community groups 119-20
community leaders 114, 120
community policing 87, 90, 94
conditions, economic 23
consumerism 24, 45-7, 71, 112, 144
consumers 69, 111, 143-5
criminal behavior 33
criminal elements 23, 33, 94-5, 107
criminal investigations 89, 91
criminal prosecution 17, 20, 44, 87
criminal trafficking cases 142
criminal violations 84-5, 95

About the Book

Erin Heil explores the global problem of human trafficking in the context of a small Florida town—one typical of the many rural communities that confront modern day slavery in their own backyards.

Drawing on two years of interviews and observation, Heil lays out the dynamics that allow both agricultural and sexual forced labor to flourish. She also highlights community antitrafficking responses. Including the perspectives of traffickers, victims, and community members in one rich portrait, her work ably contributes to the fight against human trafficking at the local, state, and national levels alike.

Erin C. Heil is assistant professor of criminal justice at Southern Illinois University Edwardsville.